OCR

D0680424

how to be a
better....
problem
solver

THE INDUSTRIAL SOCIETY

The Industrial Society stands for changing people's lives. In nearly eighty years of business, the Society has a unique record of transforming organisations by unlocking the potential of their people, bringing unswerving commitment to best practice and tempered by a mission to listen and learn from experience.

The Industrial Society's clear vision of ethics, excellence and learning at work has never been more important. Over 10,000 organisations, including most of the companies that are household names, benefit from corporate Society membership.

The Society works with these, and non-member organisations, in a variety of ways – consultancy, management and skills training, in-house and public courses, information services and multi-media publishing. All this with the single vision – to unlock the potential of people and organisations by promoting ethical standards, excellence and learning at work.

If you would like to know more about the Industrial Society please contact us.

The Industrial Society
48 Bryanston Square
London
W1H 7LN
Telephone 0171 262 2401

The Industrial Society is a Registered Charity No. 290003

how to be a better....
problem
solver

Michael Stevens

KOGAN PAGE

The Industrial Society

YOURS TO HAVE AND TO HOLD
BUT NOT TO COPY

First published in 1996, reprinted 1997

Kogan Page Limited
120 Pentonville Road
London N1 9JN

British Library Cataloguing in Publication Data
A CIP record for this book is available from the British Library.
ISBN   0 7494 1901 6

Typeset by Photoprint, Torquay, Devon
Printed in England by Clays Ltd, St Ives plc

CONTENTS

HOW TO BE A BETTER . . . SERIES

Whether you are in a management position or aspiring to one, you are no doubt aware of the increasing need for self-improvement across a wide range of skills.

In recognition of this and sharing their commitment to management development at all levels, Kogan Page and the Industrial Society have joined forces to publish the How to be a Better ... series.

Designed specifically with your needs in mind, the series covers all the core skills you need to make your mark as a high-performing and effective manager.

Enhanced by mini case studies and step-by-step guidance, the books in the series are written by acknowledged experts who impart their advice in a practical way which encourages effective action.

Now you can bring your management skills up to scratch *and* give your career prospects a boost with the How to be a Better ... series!

Titles available are:

How to be Better at Giving Presentations
How to be a Better Problem Solver
How to be a Better Interviewer
How to be a Better Teambuilder
How to be Better at Motivating People
How to be a Better Decision Maker

Forthcoming titles are:

How to be a Better Negotiator
How to be a Better Project Manager
How to be a Better Creative Thinker
How to be a Better Communicator

Available from all good booksellers. For further information on the series, please contact:

Kogan Page, 120 Pentonville Road, London N1 9JN
Tel: 0171 278 0433   Fax: 0171 837 6348

INTRODUCTION

Problem solving: transforming one set of circumstances into another, preferred state.

Every day we encounter problematic situations which cause some degree of uncertainty or difficulty in achieving the outcome we want. Resolving these situations is commonly called problem solving. It involves skills which play a fundamental role in our work, social and private lives.

People who are good at solving problems adapt more quickly in times of rapid change, they make better use of their knowledge and skills and are generally the high achievers. Problem-solving ability is therefore a major factor in determining personal success.

We have an inborn ability to solve problems, which develops rapidly as we grow and learn from experience. We become more adept at analysing situations, identifying alternative courses of action and weighing their consequences. As we learn, however, our natural ability is moulded by convention. We learn to perceive things in certain ways and to trust accepted solutions. Our thinking tends to follow well-worn paths and we shy away from the unconventional, often as a result of outside influences. Problem solving is one aspect of our biological survival mechanism and is therefore a largely unconscious process. We are generally unaware of the individual stages of problem solving and the thought processes involved. All these factors can hinder us in fully exploiting our problem-solving ability. An added problem is that many of us have not had the opportunity to learn the specific techniques available to help solve problems effectively.

This book provides practical advice on how to become a better problem solver. It will help you to:

❑ Understand the different stages of problem solving and learn to become more methodical.
❑ Recognise how your natural abilities may be hindered and learn to overcome these influences.
❑ Identify and define problems more effectively.
❑ Learn specific techniques to help with different types of problem.
❑ Generate a wider range of possible solutions.
❑ Evaluate solutions objectively to identify the most effective.
❑ Ensure that solutions are implemented properly.

Some problems can be resolved with relative ease while others present greater challenges which may require prolonged effort and concentration. Whatever the circumstances, becoming a better problem solver is rewarding in many ways. You are able to:

❑ Foresee certain problems and take preventative action.
❑ Resolve problems more quickly and with less effort.
❑ Reduce stress.
❑ Improve your work performance and working relationships.
❑ Create and exploit opportunities.
❑ Solve more demanding problems.
❑ Exert greater control over key aspects of your life.
❑ Gain greater personal satisfaction.

Using the strategies and techniques described in this book can become second nature with a little effort. Whatever your longer-term personal and professional goals, a growing sense of personal effectiveness will ensure that you gain quick payback if you make the effort.

PROBLEMS AND HOW TO SOLVE THEM

The word 'problem' refers to the uncertainties or difficulties (obstacles) encountered in getting from one situation to a preferred one (the objective). We use it loosely to describe any circumstances, real or imaginary, which we think could be improved. Problem solving is the act of bridging the gap between the two states with a course of action which achieves, or comes closer to, the desired objective. It is a process of transforming one situation into another by removing, over-coming or navigating around obstacles.

Problems can be divided broadly into two groups. *Maintenance* problems exist where the current situation is not as it should be. This may be the result of something failing to happen as expected, or something happening that should not have happened, ie there is a deviation from the 'norm'. The failure of a supplier to deliver on time and the breakdown of a production line, for example, are both maintenance problems. The second group are *achievement* problems, where the current situation could be better but there are reasons why it is not. These can be subdivided into three groups:

❑ Where the current objective has not been achieved, eg failure to achieve a sales target.
❑ Where the current objective could be exceeded, eg improving response to a sales promotion.

❏　Where an opportunity exists, eg creating a new product or service to increase sales revenues.

So problem solving is valuable in situations other than when things are not as they should be. It can help us find ways to improve performance and exploit opportunities by setting new objectives. In competitive situations it is vital that we continually improve upon the *status quo*. Innovation through problem solving helps individuals and organisations find new, more efficient ways to operate in complex and rapidly changing environments. Flexibility is essential to achieve such wide-ranging benefits. We need to understand the problem-solving process and systematically apply the skills and techniques appropriate to each problem.

THE PROBLEM-SOLVING PROCESS

Problem solving is a complex and often convoluted process which is not easily broken down into clear stages. However, there are five main sub-processes involved: recognising and defining a problem, analysing the problem, developing possible solutions, evaluating them and implementing the chosen solution. These key activities, examined in more detail later, are outlined below. Table 1.1 gives a simple example of the overall process.

Recognising and defining a problem

Problems, and opportunities, can go unnoticed unless we use appropriate techniques to detect them. Once recognised, a label or tentative definition is required to help focus our search for further information. From this we can write an accurate description or definition of the problem.

The process of definition differs for maintenance and achievement problems. With maintenance problems you need to define the norm and all the circumstances surrounding the deviation from the norm. Often this provides strong clues as to the cause.

Table 1.1 *An example of the problem-solving process*

STAGE OF PROBLEM SOLVING	EXAMPLE
Recognising the problem	Sales analysis has shown a fall in sales in the North East
Defining the problem	
Current situation	Sales in the North East have fallen by 10% in the past month
Desired situation	Sales in the North East restored to previous level at least
Objective	Restore sales in the North East to previous level plus 2% target increase within 3 months
Analysing the problem	Salesman for North East is John Davies Davies moved home 3 weeks ago New home is in South Wales Travelling time to sales area is 3 hours Davies' sales day starts at 10am and ends at 3.30pm
Possible solutions	Replace Davies in North East Offer Davies cash incentive to spend weekdays in North East Reallocate sales areas
Criteria for an ideal solution	Sales in North East restored and showing year on year growth as per target No extra cost Keep Davies in North East if possible, for his experience
Best solution	Replace Davies
Implementing the solution	John Davies offered alternative employment New salesman for North East recruited and trained
Reviewing success	John Davies resigns Sales in North East up by 15% within 6 weeks Employing new salesman incurred recruitment and training costs

Defining achievement problems involves identifying and defining the objectives and any obstacles to achieving them.

Analysing the problem

We need to fully understand problems before looking for solutions, otherwise our subsequent effort could lead us in the wrong direction. Analysing a problem involves collecting all relevant information and representing it in a meaningful way, ie so that relationships between information can be seen. Analysing maintenance problems helps to identify all possible causes and eventually confirms the real cause. With achievement problems you are looking for information which will help to suggest a range of ways to achieve the objective. This analysis also helps you decide what the ideal solution would be, which helps guide your search for solutions.

Developing possible solutions

Maintenance problems usually have one or a limited number of possible solutions. Achievement problems can often be solved in a large number of ways, the most effective being chosen from a range of possibilities. Developing solutions involves analysing the problem to ensure you fully understand it and then devising courses of action to deal with any obstacles to achieving the objective. Workable solutions are developed by combining and modifying ideas. Many techniques are available to help in this process. The more ideas you have to work with the better your chances of finding a truly effective solution.

Evaluating solutions

If there is a range of possible solutions each must be evaluated, comparing the potential outcomes, to decide which will be most effective. You need to:

❑ Identify the features of the desired outcome, including the constraints it has to meet.
❑ Eliminate solutions which do not meet the constraints.

❑ Evaluate the remaining solutions against the desired outcome.
❑ Assess the risks associated with the 'best' solution.
❑ Decide which solution to implement.

A problem is only solved when a solution has been implemented. In some situations the acceptance or agreement of others is required before implementation can take place. This may necessitate their involvement in the problem-solving process and the presentation of solutions in a favourable light.

Implementing the chosen solution

Implementation requires a plan describing the actions required to achieve the objective, time-scales and the resources required. Ways of minimising risks and preventing mistakes are also built into the plan, together with remedial actions should any stage not go as planned. As implementation progresses the effects of the actions taken are continually monitored and compared with the expected outcome. Any divergence from the expected course has to be dealt with quickly. When implementation is complete the overall success of implementation and the solution are reviewed. Further action may be required if the objective has not been achieved.

These processes provide a very flexible framework which can be applied to any problem situation. For maintenance problems the emphasis will be on defining and analysing the problem, while achievement problems require more work in generating ideas for possible solutions. There is rarely a straight path through these stages. It is generally a case of jumping back and forth amending and adapting ideas as you go. Similarly, the thinking skills used during problem solving do not follow a fixed pattern.

THINKING SKILLS

Problem solving involves mentally manipulating information using both analytical and creative thinking skills. *Analytical* or *logical* thinking includes processes such as ordering, comparing, contrasting, evaluating and selecting. It often predominates in solving maintenance problems, where several potential causes may have to be eliminated to identify the actual cause. *Creative* thinking, as the term implies, uses the imagination to create ideas. It involves looking beyond the obvious, bringing together disparate ideas and making connections to spark new ways of looking at things. There is a large element of creative thinking in solving achievement problems. It has four main dimensions:

❏ *fluency*: ease of producing ideas;
❏ *flexibility*: ease of modifying and adapting ideas;
❏ *originality*: the freshness or novelty of ideas;
❏ *elaboration*: expanding and detailing ideas.

Effective problem solving involves a mixture of analytical and creative thinking. Ideally we would be able to switch easily from one style of thinking to another. This is not always easy. Our formal education pays much more attention to the development of analytical skills and logical thinking dominates in our work. The result is that often we find it difficult to escape the analytical mind-set to a more free-flowing, creative style of thinking. However, there are techniques, described later, which help us make this switch.

Other skills are often required in solving problems effectively. Interpersonal skills, for example, may be essential where the problem or its solution involves or affects other people. The ability to work in a team, to be open to other viewpoints and to resolve conflicts constructively can all be important. The management of resources may also play a key role in both finding solutions and implementing them. This book concentrates on the thought processes involved, but other skills, knowledge and attitude are equally important in problem solving.

FAILURE TO SOLVE PROBLEMS EFFECTIVELY

Solving problems is a complex process and each of us is better able to handle some stages than others. Reasons why people fail to find effective solutions include:

❑ Not being methodical.
❑ Lack of commitment to solving the problem.
❑ Misinterpreting the problem.
❑ Lack of knowledge of the techniques and processes of problem solving.
❑ Inability to use the techniques effectively.
❑ Using a method inappropriate for the particular problem.
❑ Insufficient or inaccurate information.
❑ Inability to combine analytical and creative thinking.
❑ Failure to ensure effective implementation.

The remaining chapters of this book will help you avoid these common pitfalls. There are also other hurdles however; hidden factors of which we are often unaware. These are examined in Chapter 2.

2

HINDRANCES TO EFFECTIVE PROBLEM SOLVING

Many hidden factors hinder us in finding effective solutions to problems. Some arise from our psychological make-up, others from the environment in which we try to solve problems. You must recognise and try to counteract these influences to become better problem solvers. The influence of our working environment is examined in the next chapter. Here we concentrate on the more personal aspects of our response to problems.

How we respond to the world is shaped largely by experience. Two things can happen as a result. We may not acquire all the skills necessary to solve a particular problem and we may learn things which actually hinder us. There are four main dimensions of our psychological make-up which can be affected: perception, expression, emotion, and intellect.

PERCEPTION

Difficulties can arise when we don't accurately perceive a problem or the information needed to solve it. They include:

❑ Seeing only what we expect to see.
❑ Not recognising problems effectively.
❑ Stereotyping – applying inappropriate labels.
❑ Not seeing a problem in perspective.

The brain is very efficient at assimilating information and constructing rules about its meaning. Once these rules have been learnt we do not need full information about a situation to recognise it. We tend to rely on just the salient points or available information. We can recognise many foods from just their smell, and our friends from their voices. Often we don't look beyond the obvious. We automatically apply the most probable explanation. This is not foolproof but it works well enough – until a problem arises.

We may look at a problem, recognise a pattern of features, and instantly label it. What we are doing is relying on partial information, which can lead to mislabelling the problem and applying the wrong solution. For example, there can be more than one reason why a cheque has not been received from a customer who is often late in paying. Perhaps the invoice was not issued or did not arrive, or maybe the customer's cheque was lost in the post. It would be wrong to automatically equate non-receipt with non-payment. The same can happen in many situations.

We tend to jump to conclusions, based on the obvious, and look no further. As a result we may take too narrow a view, recognising only part of the problem or the information required to solve it. With insufficient information we may fail to see the relationships between different parts of a problem. Our solution may be inadequate because we relied only on the superficial aspects. We may fail to take account of the views of other people involved, for whom our solution is unworkable.

One particularly dangerous consequence of relying on partial information is that we simply may not recognise a problem. The introduction of new office systems may not generate complaints from staff, but that does not mean they are happy with the situation. Similarly, production targets being met does not necessarily mean that quality standards have been maintained; accounts which balance do not rule out fraud. Opportunities can also be missed when we do not see the full picture. A competitor's price rise, for example, could be exploited to win some of their business, but only when that information is recognised and linked to 'marketing opportunities'.

Of all the psychological aspects of problem solving, how we perceive situations is one of the easiest to manipulate. Following these simple steps, expanded in later chapters, will help to ensure that you see the full picture:

❑ Establish systems and procedures to alert you to potential problems and opportunities.
❑ Don't rely on single or obvious measures.
❑ Define and analyse problems carefully, ensuring you gather all relevant information.
❑ Question whether you have used inaccurate information or made assumptions about what is and isn't relevant.
❑ Ask for other people's points of view.
❑ Use graphic representations of problems to clarify the relationships between different aspects of a problem.
❑ Regularly review the *status quo*.

EXPRESSION

Difficulties with expression can include:

❑ Inability to articulate or express ideas adequately.
❑ Using the wrong 'language' to work on a problem.
❑ Unfamiliarity with the application of a language.

The ability to express information and ideas clearly during problem solving is important for our own use and for communicating with others. A common experience is to have a vague idea that seems just beyond our grasp. We are unable to clarify it in our mind because we can't find a way to describe it to ourselves. We use a wide range of 'languages', mostly words and symbols such as those used in mathematics and the sciences, to express information and articulate ideas. A single word can have enormous depth of meaning and it may have different connotations for different people. Obviously we are at a disadvantage if we lack the knowledge or skills necessary to articulate and record or communicate ideas effectively using the appropriate language.

We use words routinely to communicate and these often dominate our thinking. However, not all problems are best tackled using words alone. Explaining how to get by car from *A* to *B*, for example, is often much easier using a drawing supplemented by words. Visualisation is a very powerful tool in problem solving. In fact, using any language other than the one normally used in a particular situation can help to bring a new perspective to problems.

Often the appropriate language is dictated by the problem. For example, we wouldn't get far if a problem required quantitative analysis and we recorded data verbally. It may be dictated by our language ability. We might know a particular language but not have experience of using it in a particular way. Because we can talk does not mean we can make an effective presentation, so perhaps a written report would be a better way of communicating.

In using languages to express ideas to other people we must take account of their understanding of that language. How much do they already know and do they understand the terms you are using? This is particularly important with non-verbal languages. Communicating within a multidisciplinary team may be particularly difficult if the language is not selected carefully.

Most of us are limited in the 'languages' that we can use, but even with this restriction we can take steps to improve our expressive abilities. For example:

❑ Identify which languages are most likely to help you solve a particular problem.
❑ Get expert help with problems which necessarily involve a language you are not fluent in.
❑ Try using languages other than the norm, eg visuals instead of words, charts instead of raw data.
❑ When you explain ideas ensure that you adapt to the audience's level of understanding and use an appropriate language.

EMOTION

Our emotional make-up can cause difficulties when it conflicts with the needs of problem solving. Examples include:

❑ Fear of making mistakes or looking foolish.
❑ Impatience.
❑ Avoiding anxiety.
❑ Fear of taking risks.
❑ Need for order.

Emotion exerts an incredibly powerful influence over our thoughts and actions, even though we may regard ourselves as sober, rational individuals. It is biology again. The brain has a way of using emotions to encourage us to indulge in survival behaviour and, like much of what we think and do, this is shaped largely by our life experience. This gives rise to emotional 'needs' for achievement, recognition, order, belonging, self-esteem and so on, which differ in strength from person to person. If these needs conflict with our situation, such as a problem, we may find it difficult to act in an appropriate way. The brain may perceive it as a threat to us even though often we do not recognise it as such.

Fear of making mistakes or looking foolish in front of others is the most common manifestation of this type of emotional conflict. When we make a mistake or suggest something apparently 'silly' we expect the reaction to be ridicule. We have learnt to feel belittled by this and therefore shy away from suggesting outlandish ideas and situations where we could make mistakes. This is often more severe in the presence of colleagues of different rank. We may feel a more senior colleague thinks us inexperienced or immature, while with a junior colleague we want to protect our image of being knowledgeable and experienced. Proposing unusual ideas and risk-taking are important in problem solving.

Many people fear taking risks, where the outcome is uncertain or could be unpleasant. A major cause is our desire for security. As a result we tend to set objectives within easy reach, avoiding the risk of failure, and accept common solutions which we know will be successful. Equally damaging to problem solving, however, are a strong liking for taking risks and over-confidence that the outcome will be good.

Avoiding anxiety is another common hindrance, although some people are more susceptible to it and find it more unpleasant than others. Some people have a strong dislike of change, for example, because it introduces uncertainty which can be threatening. Common causes of anxiety include high risk, disorder and ambiguity, long-term stress and fear for our security. The effects on problem solving can include risk avoidance, indecision in ambiguous situations, excessive reliance on others' judgement and avoiding challenging the *status quo*.

A desire to reduce anxiety by bringing order to a situation, or to gain recognition through success, can make us impatient to solve a problem. The two main consequences are that we tend to grab the first plausible solution, without analysing the problem sufficiently, and we reject unusual ideas almost instinctively. Very complex problems can appear so daunting that the anxiety created makes us avoid them altogether. Conversely, a routine problem or one where the solution appears to offer little gain may not interest us at all. If it does, we are likely to choose the easiest, quickest solution.

There are many other ways in which emotion can hinder problem solving. Highly competitive people, for example, may have great difficulty is sharing ideas and also may dismiss others' ideas without consideration. A still-common fallacy is that humour, fantasy, feelings and intuition have no place in the serious business of problem solving. Subjective reports from innovators suggest otherwise. Moral codes may also exclude ideas and actions. 'Cheating' by breaking the rules is perhaps the most prevalent; sometimes rules must be broken to move ahead.

Emotion is deep-seated and an integral part of our biological being. It is not easy to change, but we can recognise and try to avoid many of the negative effects on problem solving. There are many practical steps you can take, eg:

❑ Critically question existing ideas and methods.
❑ Accept that if you are looking for new, better ways of doing something, some mistakes are almost inevitable.

❏ Remember that many people have been ridiculed for what turned out to be great inventions.

❏ If you still fear looking foolish, try to develop ideas to a practical level before showing them to others, or develop a logical argument to prove that they will work.

❏ If you dislike change, do some 'wishful thinking' to see what benefits change would bring.

❏ Follow a strictly methodical approach to curb impatience.

❏ Reduce anxiety by tackling problems in more manageable steps; if necessary, put the problem aside and come back to it later.

❏ If you do not want to take risks, identify the possible unpleasant outcomes and look for ways to minimise the risk of them happening.

❏ If a problem does not appear challenging, imagine the greatest benefits that could be achieved with a totally new solution.

INTELLECT

How we apply our intellect to problems, rather than our ability, is the primary source of difficulties. They include:

❏ Lack of knowledge or skill in the problem-solving process.
❏ Not enough creative thinking.
❏ Lack of flexibility in thinking.
❏ Not being methodical.

Knowledge, understanding and reasoning are obviously fundamental in problem solving, but however high our intellect we can all encounter difficulties applying it. The phrase: 'It's not what you've got it's how you use it', is very apt, although this obviously excludes specialist knowledge.

Probably the most common difficulties arise from lack of knowledge about the problem-solving process (the stages and skills involved) and not being able to apply the appropriate skills sufficiently well. Many of us have difficulty switching from analytical to creative thinking, for example, though we all possess the ability to be creative. Mental flexibility, such as alternating freely between visual and verbal thinking, is important. What is even more difficult is translating a creative idea into something more structured and logical, but there are techniques which can help us in these situations. We also need to know at what stage of problem solving different types of thinking skill should be applied. When should we be ordering and evaluating information and when should we give free rein to our imagination?

With practice it becomes increasingly easy to apply our minds flexibly to problems, but the following strategies can also help.

❑ Be methodical and work systematically.
❑ Consider what approach is best for each problem.
❑ Practise using the various aids to problem solving described in this book.
❑ If you do not understand the 'language' of the problem, or do not have adequate knowledge, work with someone who does.

We need to be aware constantly that how we see, feel about and react to problems is often distorted. The type and amount of distortion varies, but we must recognise when it is happening and try to avoid its adverse effects. The strategies described in this chapter can help.

3

THE WORK ENVIRONMENT

The external environment has a powerful influence on our ability to solve problems effectively. Above all, it needs to be supportive and stimulating. Our working environment presents the greatest difficulties because generally we have far less control over this than other situations. This chapter concentrates on the work environment but doubtless you will recognise factors that also have a powerful influence in the social environment.

The effect of our working environment is important for two reasons. As with the personal aspects of problem solving we need to recognise the negative influences acting on us. We are not always able to overcome or sidestep these but just recognising them can be reassuring; it is not necessarily a lack of ability which thwarts our efforts. We should also try to encourage a work environment that is more supportive of problem solving, however little control we feel we have over it.

Harnessing the potential of the whole workforce is vital to business success. This has become especially important as individual employees are empowered and become more accountable. All organisations should strive to provide an environment which supports and encourages effective problem solving. As well as the physical environment we need to consider the work policies, processes and procedures we are required to follow and the attitudes and values of those around us. These can create difficulties in many ways, eg:

❑ Inadequate physical resources to pursue new ideas.

❑ Lack of individual autonomy and responsibility.
❑ Destructive criticism of any ideas outside normal practices.
❑ Lack of recognition for improved performance through personal initiative.

PHYSICAL ENVIRONMENT

Our surroundings can have a significant effect on the way we feel, think and work. The type of environment we favour for problem solving varies, depending on what puts us in the right frame of mind for a particular task. Some people thrive in a bustling atmosphere while others prefer more sedate surroundings. Often we require different circumstances for different types of task. Quiet may be more conducive to analytical thinking, whereas lively surroundings might help us get into a more relaxed, free-thinking frame of mind. We can learn from experience what conditions suit us best for different types of mental task and then try to recreate these when needed.

Environmental stimuli determine our level of mental arousal, which affects the ease with which we can use various mental skills. Up to a certain point increasing arousal helps concentration, for example, but beyond that we are less able to concentrate. The optimum level of arousal varies for different people. Stimulation of any of the senses can affect mental arousal. The sight of flowers, the smell of coffee, the sound of traffic, etc, may raise or lower arousal depending on the individual. Emotions such as frustration and anger also affect the level of arousal.

With such a wide range of influences affecting people in different ways, there are no hard and fast rules about the best physical environment for problem solving. However, some aspects of the environment are particularly important.

Adequate resources, readily available for employees to use, are essential. Apart from providing the physical means to complete tasks, a lack of resources can cause frustration. Physical comfort is another factor, although some people may find it too soporific to be creatively stimulating. Discomfort can create a distraction, raise levels of arousal, and result in stress or lethargy. Things to consider include a comfortable, even temperature, good lighting, ergonomically designed furniture and office systems, low levels of noise and minimum through traffic. A light and airy environment, rather than a restricted enclosed workspace, has a generally beneficial effect on people's state of mind. Avoiding overcrowding, providing natural light when possible, and adequate storage facilities to minimise clutter and give the appearance of order are some of the factors to consider.

POLICIES, PROCESSES AND PROCEDURES

The way an organisation is structured, the rules and regulations which govern its operation, the channels of communication, how work processes are designed, and so on, all impact on employee performance. With the flattening of hierarchical structures and greater empowerment of the workforce, many employees now have more autonomy to make a creative contribution to the success of their organisation. Given greater accountability they are encouraged to apply their problem solving skills in their day-to-day work. With the softening of interdepartmental boundaries there are fewer barriers to sharing ideas, expertise and resources. This has happened because organisations needed to become more customer-led but it has also had the effect of enabling employees to make a fuller and more satisfying contribution. However, rules and procedures may still impose constraints and organisations must be open to changing these where it offers a better future.

Management is largely responsible for specifying and implementing policies, processes and procedures. In turn, these help to shape the organisation's culture. The effects of management and culture are examined in the next section, but often they are indistinguishable from those described here.

A good communications infrastructure supports a creative organisation only insofar as it communicates the right information to the right people. For example, employees should be sufficiently aware of business objectives, market strategies, current initiatives, and so on, to be able to apply their knowledge and skills to problems perhaps only peripherally connected to their work. When employees make a significant contribution to corporate success this must be equally well publicised, both as a reward to the individual and to encourage others.

Business process re-engineering has meant closer attention to job design to create a smoother and more efficient workflow. Many people have had their jobs enriched as a result, but it is still important to be wary of roles which involve monotonous tasks, particularly over long periods. Tedium can quickly dampen any enthusiasm for making a constructive contribution. Variation of work patterns, with regular intervals of more interesting tasks, can help.

Reward systems have a major role to play in encouraging improved performance through originality and innovation. Reward through promotion, bonuses and other cash incentives plays an important role. Suggestion schemes are a popular way of encouraging employees to contribute ideas for the successful running of a business. Often there is a financial reward, such as a share of any saving to the company when an idea is implemented.

Quality circles, described in a later chapter, are another way of encouraging employees to contribute through problem solving. Employees should also have the opportunity to suggest solutions to problems outside their own job role.

Reward comes in many forms and money is not always the most powerful incentive. Many people who leave a company to build their own business do so because their attempts to develop their ideas within the company have been frustrated. Their incentive is often achievement rather than money. Some major corporations have had success with schemes which give employees the resources to develop their ideas and build themselves a new role within the organisation.

All businesses have the opportunity to review the way they operate as organisational styles evolve. Removing constraints on originality and innovation, and finding new ways to encourage employee contribution to corporate success, are a vital component of this process.

CULTURE AND MANAGEMENT STYLE

The effective management of change has become a major issue as organisations face the challenge of adapting quickly in a turbulent commercial environment. Given the right environment the efforts of every employee can be harnessed to this end. By empowering individuals and encouraging their day-to-day contribution to solving business challenges the organisation evolves organically through the collective effort. Many factors determine the success of this approach.

Change should be seen as an opportunity rather than a threat and an adaptive response encouraged as part of the business ethic. A commitment to original thinking, aimed at finding better ways to respond in the changed environment, needs to be reflected in the business strategy and throughout its operations.

Individuals should have the expectation of high achievement through their own efforts. It is vital that this pervades the whole organisation. We tend to assume the attitude of those around us without realising. If our peers and managers are happy with the *status quo* we may easily adopt the same view.

Management style can influence both our attitude and freedom to respond creatively to changing circumstances. The classic example is when new ideas are met with a response such as, 'I don't think that's going to work, let's just keep to what we know.'

Consider the differing influence of two team leaders. One believes in leading from the front. He both suggests and implements work changes based on his own perspective, persuading other team members that this is the best course. The second team leader leads from within the team. She is always asking the others for their views, trying to get a complete picture of what's happening. When she identifies an opportunity she tells the others, 'It's time for change, where do we go from here?' She makes change a team effort. The first group of employees inevitably feel undervalued and their potential contribution is thwarted. The second team is active in building a successful business.

Anyone with responsibility for leading others, even someone asked to coach a new recruit, should encourage and help individuals to use their abilities to best effect. Delegation is one method. People with responsibility for and control over their work are more committed to working efficiently and over-coming day-to-day obstacles through their own initiative. Actively involving employees in solving non-routine problems brings further benefits. It provides experience from which they can learn and allows them to make an additional contribution. The problem is also likely to be solved more effectively. A wider perspective is available and those involved in solving a problem generally feel more committed to implementing the solution.

Setting targets and standards that stretch individuals also plays an important role. It provides a stimulating challenge, encouraging people to search for more effective ways of working, and creates an environment where individuals think only the best is acceptable. While some people find being under pressure of work or a deadline a stimulus to problem solving, others find it a hindrance. Where applicable, people should be given the opportunity to have 'time out' to tackle important problems.

Only constructive criticism creates the right atmosphere for innovative problem solving. If new ideas are shot down without consideration, particularly by more senior colleagues, people feel their extra effort is not worthwhile. More insidiously, they become over-cautious in their thinking. Original thinking is inherently risky but thought alone has no harmful effects and people should be encouraged to give free rein to their imagina-tion. When testing new ideas risk-taking should be encouraged where the consequences of failure can be tolerated.

The right atmosphere must exist to encourage people to express their ideas freely. As well as being asked for ideas on problems as they arise, people need to feel that someone will listen when they make suggestions and not be unduly critical if

Table 3.1 *Organisation and management to support problem solving*

SOME FEATURES OF SUPPORTIVE ORGANISATIONS

It is the organisation's policy to promote and support originality and innovation

People can follow their ideas through from conception to execution

Specific schemes exist to promote problem solving

People are given a large amount of autonomy and responsibility for their work

Reasonable risk-taking is encouraged

People are more concerned with good ideas than with defending their turf

Good ideas are rewarded

There are few barriers to cross-functional cooperation

Mistakes are tolerated in the cause of innovation

The organisation makes a high investment in providing good facilities and pleasant surroundings

Resources are set aside specifically for people to develop new ideas

Details of objectives and problems are made known to employees

Failure is regarded as a learning opportunity rather than an occasion for criticism

Senior management seek out new ideas in every part of the organisation

The success of individuals' ideas are reported regularly to all employees

Table 3.1 *continued*

GOOD LEADERS

Give people as much responsibility as possible

Give people freedom to organise their work as they think best

Ask people regularly for their ideas on important work issues

Get people involved in solving important problems

Continually offer encouragement to people looking for ways to improve things

Encourage people to explore hunches

Welcome suggestions for improving performance and efficiency

Put people in touch with specialists if they need help with developing ideas

Share problems with others and get their points of view

Set targets and standards that stretch people

Help people analyse situations when things go wrong rather than apportioning blame

Do not assume things could not be better because there are no problems

their ideas are unusual or seem impractical. Giving recognition for good ideas also encourages people to come forward with ideas.

The work environment exerts many different influences on problem-solving activity and different people respond to these in different ways. However, there are aspects of organisation and management which definitely encourage employees to take a more active role. These are summarised in Table 3.1.

If you find your work environment offers little support or encouragement in tackling problems there are ways you can help yourself. If there is a climate of criticism, for example, develop the strengths of your ideas and ways to overcome their weaknesses before you propose them. Being careful how you explain your ideas to others will also help to avoid premature criticism. When the atmosphere at work is not conducive to tackling problems set aside time to work on them elsewhere. If your work is monotonous, introduce some variety by looking for different ways of doing the job, or look for varied tasks that could be delegated to you. When people may be reluctant to provide the help you need, try to identify the benefits to them of solving the problem before you ask for help.

Ultimately all employees have an impact on their work environment. Consider how you affect those around you and whether you could make things better for them.

4

WHAT IS THE PROBLEM?

Problems are not always obvious, tangible things. Sometimes they are obscured by circumstances or have little immediate impact. They may change over time, becoming more or less important or even disappearing altogether. Before you tackle a problem you need to identify it, discover precisely what it is and decide whether it needs to be solved now, later or not at all.

RECOGNISING PROBLEMS

Some problems arise suddenly, without warning, and are obvious by their effects. Others develop slowly and have a more subtle influence. Sometimes what appears to be a problem turns out not to be a problem at all. We need methods to help us recognise potential problems as early as possible.

CASE STUDY

Three months into a major new works building programme several suppliers refuse to supply any more materials until their earlier invoices have been paid. One person in a department is responsible for processing supplier invoices before they are passed to accounts for payment. When the building programme began that person's workload escalated dramatically. By giving priority to invoices for essential production supplies, building suppliers were waiting much longer than usual for payment. Eventually there was a two-month backlog and the suppliers' reaction to the delay was understandable.

This example highlights how some problems develop. The objective here was to efficiently process invoices for goods supplied. It went through phases – latent (after supply of goods but before an invoice arrived), current (after an invoice had arrived and before it was passed to accounts), then latent again (once an invoice was passed to accounts and before the next arrived). Similarly, the obstacle or cause (the lack of resources or failure to process invoices efficiently) went through phases. It was developing, though latent, when a large number of invoices began arriving from building suppliers. It became effective when a delay developed in processing their invoices and would have become latent again when the employee caught up with the backlog.

All objectives and obstacles go through phases to some extent. A problem arises when a current objective coincides with an effective obstacle. The growth and decay of objectives and obstacles varies tremendously. An employee's dissatisfaction with his job may have been growing for many months or even years before he chooses to resign; annual sales targets are achieved gradually over 12 months and may undergo seasonal and monthly variations; brake linings on a car wear until brake failure could potentially cause an accident.

If you can monitor the growth and decay of objectives and potential obstacles you can often take action to prevent a problem occurring, or at least be prepared to tackle it immediately it arises. Recognising problems efficiently involves being aware of the areas in which they may arise and establishing specific methods of detection. Monitoring performance, for example, enables you to detect any shortfall in achieving targets and standards. Observing and listening to others helps to detect changes which may reflect an underlying problem. Regularly reviewing and comparing past performance and behaviour with the current situation highlights any deterioration. It is important not to jump to conclusions about apparent problems and possible causes until you have investigated further and defined the problem effectively.

Recognising opportunities for improvement also benefits from a systematic approach. Ask yourself if current targets could be exceeded, whether you could utilise resources more efficiently, and whether there are new objectives to be achieved. You can ask the same questions of colleagues at work and even other departments, looking for opportunities in terms of both performance and the needs of employees.

A major area for identifying new objectives for business is the marketplace. What does the market need that we could supply? In a sense you are looking at other people's problems that you could solve, either by supplying a new product or service or improving an existing one. The most direct way to identify market needs is to approach customers and prospects. What problems do they have with existing products or services? What needs do they have that you could meet with a new product or service?

When you recognise a problem, or an opportunity, you need to identify whose responsibility it is, ie who 'owns' it. If a problem is not your direct responsibility you will need to inform the owner. You may be asked to deal with it anyway, but the owner may have the information or resources needed to find a solution, or you may need the owner's approval to implement your solution.

DEFINING PROBLEMS

The first sign that a problem exists is often a hazy notion that things are not as they should be, or that they could be better. To deal with the situation effectively you need to describe or define it as something you can act upon. Problem definitions vary in complexity but their primary function is to point you in the right direction for further work on the problem. The definition helps to:

❑   Identify a tangible target to be achieved.

❑ Reduce complex problems to a series of smaller problems.
❑ Focus on the important aspects of a problem.
❑ Assess its importance and allocate appropriate resources to solve it.
❑ Explain the problem to others who may be involved or can help in its solution.
❑ Locate clues to possible strategies and solutions.
❑ Define the type of information you require.
❑ Define criteria for measuring the potential effectiveness of various solutions.

To define a problem effectively you need information. The method by which the problem was detected provides enough information to make a preliminary definition. You might have noticed in the monthly sales report, for example, that sales have fallen in one region. This tells you what type of further information you need and where to look for it. Often you need to redefine a problem, perhaps several times, as your understanding of it grows.

Maintenance and achievement problems are usually defined in different ways. With maintenance problems, where finding a solution first involves finding the cause, there is more emphasis on identifying and specifying the possible causes. Achievement problems, where there are many possible solutions, require a definition which broadens the search for solutions. Defining maintenance problems is an analytical, convergent (narrowing) process. Defining achievement problems is a more creative, divergent (expansive) process.

Maintenance problems

Defining maintenance problems involves identifying and recording all aspects of the deviation from the norm, from which you can begin to identify possible causes. Your preliminary definition might be, 'The delinquency (failure to pay) rate on debts has risen by 5 per cent over the past month.' This type of definition is of little help in locating the cause of such a problem (in this case primarily a rise in the mortgage rate), but it's a starting point for making a detailed description of the situation.

One technique used for defining maintenance problems is the Kepner-Tregoe approach, which helps to systematically analyse and define all the circumstances surrounding the problem. It consists of answering a series of questions such as:

- ❑ What is the problem?
- ❑ What isn't the problem?
- ❑ Where is the problem?
- ❑ Where isn't the problem?
- ❑ What is distinctive about it?
- ❑ Who/what does the problem involve?
- ❑ Who/what doesn't the problem involve?
- ❑ When did/when does the problem occur?
- ❑ When didn't/when doesn't it occur?
- ❑ What is the same when the problem occurs?
- ❑ What is different when the problem occurs?
- ❑ What is the extent of the problem?
- ❑ Is the problem getting bigger/smaller?
- ❑ What is distinctive about its change in size?

Questions can be adapted to the situation so that all known facts about the problem are identified and documented. A notable feature is that it asks questions such as, 'What isn't the problem?' and 'When doesn't the problem occur?' The method is very thorough and involves extensive analysis. Once the situation has been fully documented, possible causes may be apparent. These are tested against the known facts and the actual cause is the one which would have precisely the effects documented. Often other possible causes have to be hypothesised and tested. Creative thinking may play an important role here, perhaps using models to represent the problem and idea generation techniques (both examined in later chapters).

The Kepner-Tregoe method can also be used to identify potential problems by asking, 'What could go wrong?' The most serious problems with the highest probability of occurring are identified and documented in terms of possible causes and how these could be prevented or dealt with.

Once the actual cause of a maintenance problem is identified the action required to solve it may be obvious and straightforward. On other occasions it may be necessary to define the problem in terms of objectives and obstacles, like achievement problems, and use the appropriate techniques to develop possible solutions.

Achievement problems

Achievement problems are defined in terms of goals or objectives (what you want to achieve by solving the problem) and obstacles standing in the way. The definition needs to be precise, to give clear direction to your search for solutions, but at the same time to identify all possible goals that would contribute to your overall objective. Achievement problems often don't have a single 'correct' definition, so they are best defined in two stages – first to explore all the possible goals and then to define precisely those you want to achieve. Then the obstacles are added.

'How to . . . ?' statements are useful when focusing attention on the problem area and provide a basis for suggesting alternative goals and routes to a solution. 'How to increase sales?', for example, could be restated as:

How to make our product more saleable?

. . . increase sales outlets?

. . . make our marketing more effective?

. . . increase our market share?

. . . make our sales team more effective?

All of these goals suggest different ways of helping to achieve the first stated objective. There is usually more than one way of looking at a problem. What appears to be a single problem may in fact be a collection of related problems. If you define the problem solely as having too much work to do, for example, you might consider delegation as the only solution. If you defined it also as having too little time to complete your work, a new avenue (better time management) opens up. Some of the techniques examined in Chapters 5 and 6 can be used to help identify alternative 'How to . . .?' statements and goals.

The more precise the definition, the greater your chances of finding an effective solution. 'How to improve my efficiency?' gives little information about the situation and does not tell you where to look for solutions. This could be divided into a series of statements such as 'How, within three months, to complete reports in three days instead of the five it takes me now', and 'How, within six months, to reduce the average time I spend in meetings each week from twelve hours to eight.' These statements clearly define the situation now, the goal, and the gap that needs to be bridged in solving the problem.

The same is true of statements about obstacles. The more clearly they are defined the easier it is to find ways to deal with them. Asking yourself questions about the obstacles will help you define them, eg:

❑   What is the obstacle?

❏ How did/does it arise?

_____

_____

_____

_____

❏ What are its dimensions?

_____

_____

_____

_____

❏ What are its effects?

_____

_____

_____

_____

❏ Is it growing or diminishing?

_____

_____

_____

_____

❑   Is it temporary or permanent?

✎ _____

_____

_____

_____

To write your detailed definition, first select the 'How to ...?' statements which most accurately represent the problem. Then, for each one, write down the characteristics of the current situation and the desired situation. Whenever possible these characteristics should be stated in measurable terms, so that you know what will constitute a successful solution, when it should be achieved, and how you will measure your success. Next, add details of any obstacles and how they prevent you reaching your objective. A simple example is given in Table 4.1.

Your definition will form the basis for analysing the problem and searching for solutions (see Chapter 5).

It is important to consider how changing the current situation into the desired one would affect others. One of the objectives of a manager wanting to manage his time more effectively, for example, may be to spend less time 'walking the job'. This means less direct contact with staff, less opportunity for observation and less time to discuss their concerns. Depending on the situation, you can either modify your objectives or set secondary objectives to accommodate the needs of others. This manager, for example, might institute a regular 'surgery' for discussions with staff. Differences in needs can also be reconciled through negotiation or use of authority (with caution!).

You can use the following checklist to review how thoroughly you have defined a problem.

❑   Can this objective be divided into several sub-goals?
❑   Is this objective the ultimate goal in solving the problem?

Table 4.1 *Defining an achievement problem*

HOW TO . . .?

Some of the statements listed were

1. How to make better use of sales information?
2. How to spot sales trends more quickly?
3. How to provide sales analysis as soon as possible after month end?
4. How to learn more about customer buying habits?

Statement 3 was used to define the problem as follows

CURRENT SITUATION
End of month figures received by fax from salespeople 3 days after month end

Data entry onto office PC network takes half a day

Analysis of data takes half a day

Sales analysis completed the fourth day after month end

DESIRED SITUATION
Sales analysis completed the day after month end

CHANGES REQUIRED
End of month figures made available for analysis the morning after month end

Reduce data entry time

OBSTACLES
Salespeople record sales on forms after each appointment

They tend to transfer figures from the forms to their home PCs (which takes time) all together after month end

The compiled figures are faxed to the office in the evening and need to be entered onto the office PC network ready for analysis

- [ ] Is achieving this objective simply a route to achieving another objective?
- [ ] Are there other related objectives?
- [ ] Can this obstacle be sub-divided?
- [ ] Does this obstacle really prevent me reaching this objective?
- [ ] Are there other related obstacles?
- [ ] Does this obstacle prevent me reaching other objectives?
- [ ] Does this definition take account of the needs of others who are involved or who may be affected?

Many of the techniques described here for defining achievement problems can also be applied to maintenance problems once their cause has been identified. Sometimes the process of defining a problem reveals that it does not require action, perhaps because it will disappear and not recur, or because the actual loss or potential gain is relatively insignificant. On other occasions you need to decide when it would be best to act.

IS ACTION NECESSARY, AND WHEN?

The effects of some problems are not significant enough to merit time and effort in solving them. Even when they do, because many objectives and obstacles go through phases of growth and decay, tackling a problem immediately may not be the best course of action. There are four main options when you encounter a problem:

1. *Do nothing*: eg when the problem will solve itself; when its effects are insignificant; when the cost of solving it is greater than the potential gains.

2. *Monitor the situation*: eg when it is not urgent; when the problem is diminishing; when you are unsure of the cause; when you need time to plan what to do; when the obstacle is getting smaller; when the objective is developing or declining and finding a solution is likely to be difficult.

Table 4.2 *Deciding whether to act now or wait*

What is the extent of the benefits offered by solution?			What is the extent of the losses if I don't act?
What are the chances of the benefits diminishing?			What are the chances of the benefits growing?
At what rate will they diminish?			At what rate will they grow?
What are the chances of the losses growing?			What are the chances of the losses diminishing?
At what rate will losses grow?			At what rate will losses diminish?
ACT			WAIT

3. **Deal with the effects**: eg when the cause will subside; when the cost of removing the cause is too great; when an obstacle is too intractable.

4. **Try to solve it immediately**: eg when the problem is growing; when it is having serious effects; when the obstacle is getting larger; when the objective is developing or declining and finding a solution is likely to be relatively easy; when a deadline has been imposed.

You can use the grid in Table 4.2 to help you to decide whether to act now or to wait. Apply each question to the problem and score the answers as high (3), medium (2) or low (1). The highest scoring column indicates whether you should act now or wait. Although this grid can be used accurately in many situations, there may be overriding factors which you need to consider, such as deadlines imposed by internal or external authorities.

This grid can also be used when you face several problems which all appear to need your immediate attention. If some of the problems cannot be delegated to others then you need to tackle them in order of priority. The score in the left-hand column will tell you the relative urgency of acting on each problem. There may be overriding factors, of course, such as one problem having to be solved first to facilitate the solution of another.

When you have decided to act on a problem, the search for solutions involves finding ways to close the gap between your current situation and one where you will have achieved your objective. At any stage it may be necessary to redefine the problem. Or you may decide that, due to new information or a change in circumstances, the problem does not require further action.

5

DEVISING SOLUTIONS

Devising solutions to problems can be the most exciting part of problem solving. Achievement problems in particular give you the opportunity to let your imagination run riot.

Some problems require no further analysis once they have been defined effectively. The definition of a maintenance problem, for example, might confirm that a particular component has failed in the manufacturing plant. Replacing that component solves the problem. More complex problems require further analysis to help identify how to bridge the gap between the current and desired situations. Achievement problems generally require most work at this stage.

Before starting more detailed work on a problem, decide if you should involve others. These may be people who are part of the problem or affected by it, with experience or knowledge of this type of problem, or people with the necessary resources. There is a list of questions on page 78 which will help you decide if a group problem-solving approach would be best.

Getting from your definition of the problem to an acceptable solution involves:

❑ Analysing and exploring the problem:
  – identifying, gathering and recording relevant information;
  – representing the information in a meaningful way using 'models'.
❑ Defining criteria of effectiveness for solutions.
❑ Devising solutions.

The relative importance of these processes can vary according to the problem and they are usually interdependent, so that you move back and forth as you progress towards finding acceptable solutions.

EXPLORING AND ANALYSING THE PROBLEM

Thorough information forms the basis for developing effective solutions. It is vital to distinguish between facts, ideas, needs and opinions, although they may all be important. A significant number of employees may all express the same need, for example, which must be accommodated within the solution.

Analysing maintenance problems using the Kepner-Tregoe method (page 39) may result in a vast amount of information about the situation. This must be analysed to eliminate causes that do not fit the facts. As the number of possible causes is reduced more information about the remaining possibilities is often required. If you find that the problem only exists when a particular team is working on a project, for example, you need more information to locate the problem within that team. Are specific members of the team implicated? If more than one, is it a problem of relationships? Through a cyclical process of investigation and elimination you eventually identify the actual cause.

The definition of achievement problems (see Table 4.1, page 44, for example) gives clues about what is relevant – objectives, obstacles, the current and desired situations – and where that information might be found. The following questions can be useful when gathering information:

❑ What class of information is required, eg financial, technical, policy, behavioural, strategic?

✎
_____

_____

_____

_____

❏ What specific information is required, eg dates, times, amounts, names, actions?

_____

_____

_____

_____

❏ Why is this information required, eg to eliminate possibilities, to confirm hunches, to identify resources for solving the problem?

_____

_____

_____

_____

❏ What are the sources of this information, eg yourself, colleagues, eye-witnesses, records, specialists, other departments, books, researchers?

_____

_____

_____

_____

❏ What form will it take, eg numerical, statistical, verbal, physical?

✎

_____

_____

_____

_____

❏ How accurate or reliable are the sources, eg are they biased, is the information in the form of opinions or statistical analyses?

✎

_____

_____

_____

_____

❏ How can this information be obtained, eg memos, reports, meetings, informal discussions, observation, listening, testing?

✎

_____

_____

_____

_____

Many of the methods for representing problems described later, and the idea generation techniques examined in the next chapter, can help identify information potentially relevant to solving both achievement and maintenance problems.

Try to gather and record information systematically. If necessary, verify the original source and how and when it was gathered. Remember that numerical and statistical data can be manipulated to serve vested interests. Try to ensure that the way information is presented to you reflects the true situation and that any conclusions offered about its relevance are accurate and logical.

A crucial aspect of problem solving, especially with complex problems, is how you organise and represent information. Two very common difficulties in problem solving are not seeing all the relationships between different parts of the problem and not seeing beyond the most obvious solution. With complex problems it is often impossible to hold all the information in your mind and think about it clearly. Even with simpler problems it helps to have a tangible representation, or model, of the problem which gives structure to the information. Models help to:

❏ Reveal relationships between different aspects of the problem.
❏ Highlight gaps in your information and understanding.
❏ Stimulate your search for solutions.
❏ Communicate understanding to other people.
❏ Predict the likely consequences of actions you think might solve the problem.

Models give shape and structure to information, making it easier to remember, think about and build on our ideas. There are many different types, composed variously of words, graphics, mathematical formulae, symbols, as well as physical models.

Various standard models are used to represent problems that have common elements linked by the same relationships. These can be applied to any problem that fits the model. Chemical equations and algebraic formulae are examples. So are business 'games', which represent details of a variety of business situations and predict the consequences of our actions according to the rules of the 'real' world. Another example is communication, where the common elements are the originator, the sender, the message, the medium and the receiver. Effective communication relies on an efficient flow of information from one end to the other. This model can be used to analyse communication in a particular situation and identify exactly what's happening at each stage. Some other types of model are described below.

Words as models

Words are the simplest and one of the most popular and flexible ways of representing a problem, either alone or in combination with pictorial or graphical elements. The easiest way to create a word model is to list the main features of a problem, perhaps including associated ideas that spring to mind. This can be updated and expanded as you think of additional relevant information. Word models can be manipulated, reordering words in sequence or classifying them into groups, to highlight the relationships and differences between the information.

Abbreviated notes can be used effectively in the same way. Prose, however, which is often used to describe a problem, is less effective. This is because the more structure that exists the less easy it is to add to and manipulate the information to reveal new relationships.

Words are easy to record and they act as potent stimuli to the imagination. They are the most common way of communicating problems to other people. There are some drawbacks, however. The choice of a particular word or phrase to describe an idea can obscure its relationship with other relevant information. If you use the word 'box' to describe a 'container' you want to redesign, for example, the description could narrow your thinking about different shapes and materials. Giving structure to information in word models can also be difficult. It's therefore a good idea to use them in combination with other types of model.

Drawings and diagrams

Drawing is an ideal way of beginning to create some kind of structure with your ideas. Unlike words alone, lines and shapes can represent relationships more easily and give concrete form to a problem. Drawings can suggest new relationships between ideas, new ways of structuring a problem and new routes to a solution.

In drawing a representation of a problem you are not trying to specify it precisely. It should be more spontaneous, allowing your thoughts to evolve in a visual way.

Mind maps

The use of 'mind maps' to boost creativity and problem-solving ability has been written about and developed extensively by Tony Buzan. It's a method of recording ideas which stimulates creative thinking. It also brings structure to ideas relating to a problem even though it relies on spontaneity.

The main idea or concept is written down and related ideas are added, as they spring to mind, as branches off a central point. Each idea is labelled so that it acts as a trigger for recalling associated ideas which are added as connecting lines, branching out in all directions. The method capitalises on the brain's power of association so it should be spontaneous, without thinking of where to place branches, whether to exclude an idea, or thinking of ways of extending a particular branch if nothing springs to mind. Branches are not limited to straight lines. A wavy line might represent fluctuation, for example, and an expanding spiral something escalating out of control. Anything which gives stronger representation to the idea helps to trigger the recall of associated ideas.

No structure is imposed consciously but relationships emerge through the association of ideas. Moving outwards from the main idea reveals its relationships with other, often very remote ideas. Mind mapping becomes easier with practice and is very effective, both for representing the ramifications of a problem and generating ideas for solutions.

Chain diagrams

Chain diagrams are created in a more logical way than mind maps and show how the main elements of a problem are related (like a flowchart). You could show the stages in the manufacture of a product or the supply of a service, for example, with the materials, labour and time involved at each stage. They can be very complicated, with many parallel processes, multiple branching and feedback loops. The direction of 'flow' of the process can be represented by arrows and numbers added to quantify what is happening at each stage.

Chain diagrams can also be used to show the alternative choices that can be made in the system and the influence of chance events. This forms what is sometimes called a tree diagram. When numbers are added to show the value of alternative choices and the probability of chance events a decision tree is created, which can be used to evaluate alternative courses of action. The fault-tree diagram, represented in Figure 5.1, is another variation which helps to identify faults in a system. This type of diagram can be used as a basis for investigating the causes of a problem, starting with those which have the highest probability.

Force-field diagrams

Force-field diagrams are analytical tools for representing the dynamics of situations and suggesting ways of influencing the forces and pressures which create and maintain them.

Creating a force-field diagram involves identifying and representing graphically the equilibrium between two opposing sets of forces, as illustrated in Figure 5.2. Applied to problem solving the driving forces are those which would push the equilibrium in the direction needed to achieve the objective. The opposing or restraining forces are those which act against the desired change – the obstacles to achieving the objective.

To push the equilibrium in the direction needed to achieve the objective you need to find ways of overcoming or neutralising the restraining or opposing forces, and/or strengthening the driving forces. Force-field analysis can be divided into simple stages:

1. Describe the current situation.
2. Describe the objective or desired outcome.

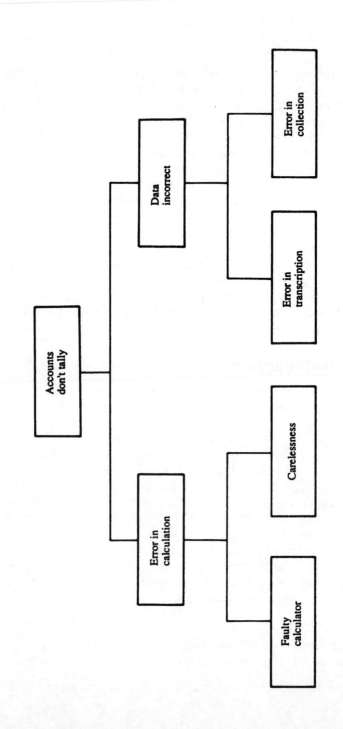

Figure 5.1 *Example of a fault-tree diagram*

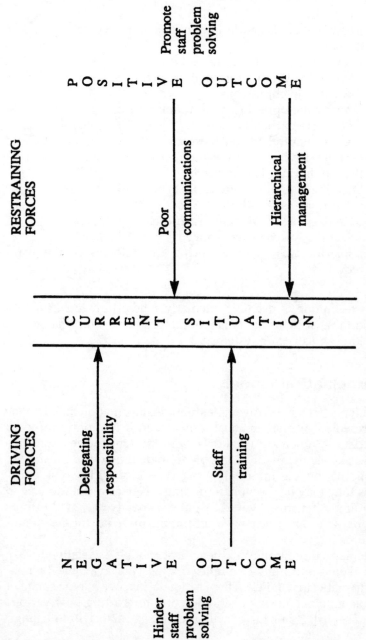

RESTRAINING FORCES

Promote staff problem solving

POSITIVE OUTCOME

Poor communications

Hierarchical management

CURRENT SITUATION

DRIVING FORCES

Delegating responsibility

Staff training

NEGATIVE OUTCOME

Hinder staff problem solving

Figure 5.2 *Example of a force-field diagram*

3. Describe the least desired outcome (a worsening of the problem).
4. Draw the basic diagram.
5. Identify the driving forces (those acting to push equilibrium towards the objective).
6. Identify the opposing or restraining forces.
7. Add these to the diagram.
8. Identify neutral forces; these are not active now but could become driving or opposing forces when action is taken or the equilibrium is disturbed.
9. Describe individual forces in detail and rate their relative importance/strength.
10. Rate the ease of changing each force.
11. Select the forces to be changed.
12. Look for ways of influencing these forces in the ways required.

This technique is useful particularly where human factors are important, such as in behavioural problems and changes in working practices or systems.

Mathematical models

Problems which involve quantitative information need to be represented in mathematical terms, even if it is only to record the data. Mathematical models can represent the relationships between elements of a problem and provide a means of manipulating the information, eg $A + B = C$. In some situations they may be essential in finding an effective solution, eg in deciding what stress would be put on a newly designed turbine before you can select an appropriate material for its manufacture.

Constructing simple mathematical models is relatively easy but even some highly complex models are available to non-mathematicians on PCs. These can help to solve a large range of problems by analysing a situation and forecasting how various actions, changes or forces will affect it, eg financial modelling.

Using an appropriate model to represent a problem will often suggest some ideas for a solution. There are more powerful techniques for generating ideas, however, which are described in Chapter 6.

By this stage you should have a detailed understanding of the problem. If you are dealing with a maintenance problem you may have thought of more possible causes and gathered the information supporting or refuting each cause. Idea-generation techniques may be used to identify still further possible causes. The search continues until, by a process of elimination, the actual cause is identified as the one which has precisely the same effects as those which have occurred.

DEFINING CRITERIA OF EFFECTIVENESS

Before developing solutions you need to know what will constitute an effective solution. Many factors are involved. An effective solution must:

❑ Provide an acceptable level of benefits in terms of the objective.
❑ Deal effectively with obstacles/causes.
❑ Meet constraints on time, space, human resources and materials.
❑ Be cost effective and affordable.
❑ Be acceptable to:
  – those affected by the problem and the solution, eg employees, customers, clients, suppliers;
  – those who have to agree the solution;
  – those who will provide the necessary resources;
  – those who have to implement the solution.
❑ Involve an acceptable level of risk.

You need to make a detailed list of what you want to achieve and what factors must be taken into account within your solution. In some of these areas there will be both 'acceptable' and 'ideal' outcomes and you can define both. These 'criteria of effectiveness' give direction to your search for solutions and will help you later to compare the relative effectiveness of possible solutions (see Chapter 8). The criteria are not set in stone, however, because you may find a solution which warrants changing the constraints. For example, you may have a budget of £4000 to reduce job completion time by 10 per cent. If you find a solution that would achieve a 25 per cent reduction but requires a larger budget then the extra spend may be justified.

DEVISING SOLUTIONS

Devising solutions involves constructing courses of action which meet your criteria of effectiveness as closely as possible. However, these can inhibit idea generation. The best approach is to create as many ideas as possible for achieving your objectives and test them against these criteria once you've explored all the possibilities.

Analysing the problem should have provided a large amount of information and possible ideas to work with. The objective of the problem defined in Table 4.1 (page 44), for example, was to complete monthly sales analyses the day after month end instead of the fourth day. The definition highlighted the major bottleneck as salespeople waiting until month end to transfer sales information from paper forms onto their home PCs before they faxed it to the office. They can only do this after work and it takes at least two evenings.

Looking at the problem this way, the obvious solution is to ensure that salespeople update their home PCs regularly. However, they say this is not always practical and it is much less of a burden to transfer all the information together. Looking at the problem again we see that they are recording daily the sales information on forms. Using laptop PCs to record this information, instead of paper forms, would remove the obstacle of having to transfer it later. Obviously cost would be a major constraint but the solution has major advantages.

Salespeople would be maintaining a day-to-day record of sales using a laptop PC. Cumulative sales figures could be downloaded to the office PC at any time, on a daily basis if required. It would also make it easy for salespeople to record ad-hoc customer comments, such as their reasons for placing a larger or smaller order than usual and their feedback on different products and the company's service. With laptop PCs the sales team could provide more information more quickly.

Recall the original 'How to . . . ?' statements listed in Table 4.1:

❑ How to make better use of sales information?
❑ How to spot sales trends more quickly?
❑ How to provide sales analysis as soon as possible after month end?
❑ How to learn more about customer buying habits?

We now see that the benefits of providing laptop PCs contribute to achieving all of the original goal statements in one way or another. The cost of this solution may therefore be justified.

Continually questioning your view of the situation as you search for solutions will help you to explore all the possibilities. For example, ask yourself:

❑ Do I really need to achieve this objective?

_____

_____

_____

_____

❑ Could I substitute a different objective?

_____

_____

_____

_____

❑ Could I achieve this objective in a different way?

_____

_____

_____

_____

❑ Would there be any advantage in delaying trying to achieve this objective?

_____

_____

_____

_____

❑ Would someone else be more effective in achieving this objective?

_____

_____

_____

_____

❑ Is this really an obstacle?

_____

_____

_____

_____

❏ Would someone else be more effective in dealing with this obstacle?

✎

_____

_____

_____

_____

❏ Can I deal with the causes of this obstacle?

✎

_____

_____

_____

_____

❏ Can I side-step this obstacle?

✎

_____

_____

_____

_____

❏ Can I use this obstacle to my advantage?

✎

_____

_____

_____

_____

As you construct different plans of action you can use an appropriate model to represent how each action contributes to achieving your overall objective. Models also help you predict the effects of various actions and to see how they interact. It is important that the actions form a coherent strategy for tackling the problem. When several actions have to run consecutively, for example, you need to ensure that together they will meet any time constraints that exist, and that there are no conflicting demands on resources. These factors will become apparent when you are evaluating your solutions (see Chapter 8).

Each action that you propose will be intended to achieve a particular effect. In doing so it may also have side-effects which can be desirable or undesirable. Once you have formulated a possible solution you should try to build into it ways to minimise undesirable side-effects and to capitalise on the desirable ones. Introducing new technology to improve efficiency, for example, may necessitate training. In turn, this could be an opportunity to reorganise associated out-dated processes and procedures. Similarly, an in-store promotion can be used to positively influence public perceptions of the company at the same time as promoting the product.

You need to identify all the factors that could influence the effectiveness of your solution. Asking the following types of question will help.

❏ What could go wrong, eg does the person you are relying upon to negotiate the contract have enough experience?

_____

_____

_____

_____

❏ Are there related factors over which I have no control, eg government legislation, internal policy changes?

✎

_____

_____

_____

_____

❏ Could this objective change, eg are higher targets likely to be set before this solution is implemented?

✎

_____

_____

_____

_____

❏ Could this obstacle become more intractable, eg with the imminent reorganisation of the department could this person become even more uncooperative?

✎

_____

_____

_____

_____

❏ Could relevant new obstacles arise, eg a change in market needs, a competitor using the same solution?

✎
_____

_____

_____

_____

❏ Might this action create a new opportunity which could be exploited at the same time, eg could we market some of the information on this new database and offset some of our costs?

✎
_____

_____

_____

_____

When you have a number of solutions that you feel could achieve your objective effectively you have to evaluate them. This process is explained in Chapter 8.

6

IDEA-GENERATION TECHNIQUES

The major difficulty in generating new ideas to help solve problems is escaping the habitual ways we associate information. This 'logic of experience' hinders us in combining information in unusual ways. We find it hard to see common situations in a new light. The linking of disparate pieces of information and ideas that appear irrelevant may be consciously excluded or not triggered from memory because of their weak association with the situation. The result is that we fail to explore all possible routes to a solution. The techniques described in this chapter help to overcome these restrictions.

DIFFERENT TECHNIQUES

There are many different techniques that can help to generate new ideas, some relying on mental strategies and others utilising more mechanical methods. The emphasis is on the quantity of ideas produced rather than the quality. This gives a large number of ideas to use in devising solutions, which subsequently can be evaluated.

An important element in using nearly all of these techniques is suspension of judgement, which means deliberately avoiding any type of evaluation. Evaluating ideas puts a brake on the imagination and inhibits the mind in making unusual and potentially useful connections. Sometimes it's easy to come up with unusual or radical ideas, for example when we know we are only 'playing'. However, as soon as we face a serious task we exclude these ideas, either consciously or unconsciously, simply because they are not commonly associated with a practical solution.

During idea generation you should try to think in a playful way by deliberately suspending judgement. A useful warm-up is to do a fluency exercise to get you in the right frame of mind.

Fluency exercises

Fluency is the ease of producing ideas. There are many simple playful exercises for the imagination which can help to improve fluency. Although this improvement is not always permanent, these exercises are very useful as a warm-up for other, more productive idea-generation techniques. In group problem solving they serve the additional purpose of overcoming individuals' reticence to voice unusual ideas.

Fluency exercises are typically simple and require you to write down as many ideas as possible in a short time, usually a minute or two. One example is to select a common object and list as many possible uses for it as you can think of in that time. Another example is to think of a bizarre situation and write down all the consequences you can think of, eg what would happen if you woke up one morning and everything relying on electricity had ceased to function?

Flexibility of thinking is also revealed in these exercises. The more wide-ranging the ideas the more flexible your thinking. Fluency and flexibility tend to increase with practice, so when you have a couple of minutes to relax, these exercises can be fun and worthwhile.

Free association

This technique consists of allowing the mind to wander without deliberate direction. You name the first thing that comes to mind in response to a trigger word, symbol, idea or picture, then use that as a trigger, quickly repeating the process over and over to produce a stream of associations. The important thing is to avoid justifying the connection between successive ideas. This encourages spontaneity and the emergence of ideas only marginally related to the trigger word.

Free association delves deep into the memory, helping you to discover remote relationships similar to those uncovered using mind maps. To be productive, the ideas need to be recorded, either in writing or on audio tape. This can interfere with the free flow of ideas and therefore requires practice.

Discussion

A very simple way of getting additional ideas is to discuss the problem with other people. They will often have a different perspective on the problem and its implications, and different values and ideals. Even if they can't directly contribute significant ideas, what they say may trigger new lines of thought for you. Discussing your problem with other people is a very valuable supplement to other idea-generation techniques.

Daydreaming

Daydreaming is frowned upon and actively discouraged as a serious thinking skill, being labelled as fanciful, indulgent and unproductive. In fact it is one of the basic thinking tools of all good problem solvers. It has several important qualities:

❏ The label 'daydreaming' helps you to think in terms of time out for playful, uninhibited thinking.
❏ It can be fitted into spare moments.
❏ It involves only thoughts not actions, so there is no risk.
❏ It's private, so you are not open to ridicule by others.
❏ It often involves feelings and emotions which add a valuable dimension to your thinking.
❏ Ideas can be manipulated quickly and potential obstacles foreseen.
❏ Rewards can be envisaged clearly and act as a motivator.

❑ It helps to develop plans which prepare you to look out for information and opportunities to help you achieve objectives.

Productive daydreaming has to be directed towards a particular goal and is often called wishful thinking. There is no crime in wishing for the apparently impossible. Inventors do it all the time. If you set your sights high you can use daydreaming to help you build plans for achieving your goals.

Visualising

This involves thinking about a problem in visual terms. It can be useful in solving many types of problem. If you had to devise a formula for measuring the amount of carpet required to cover a spiral staircase, for example, you would probably automatically picture the staircase in your mind. From there you would start to devise ways to make the calculation based on the shape of the steps. In other situations the choice may not be so obvious, but visualising is a very powerful and flexible way of thinking about problems and it can be developed with practice.

Incubation

When you get stuck with a problem after working on it for some time it is often productive to take a break from it. Once we have absorbed all the relevant information and stop work on a problem it appears that the mind continues to manipulate the information, unconsciously looking for relevant relationships and patterns. Often a new idea or even a solution will spring to mind after this period of incubation.

The phrase 'sleep on it' has arisen because sleep is an enforced period of incubation. There are many reports of people awaking with new insights to a problem they have been working on. Kekulé, the German chemist, is said to have discovered the ring structure of benzene after dreaming of a snake biting its tail. When time allows, putting aside a problem for a while can help in giving you a new perspective, if not a solution.

Checklists

These are lists of thought-provoking questions. They can prompt the search for specific information and stimulate ideas. Idea-generation checklists work by asking what the result would be if you manipulated information in a particular way. They can be used on ideas or objects and have been developed to serve various purposes. One well-known example, the *Check List for New Ideas*, developed by Alex Osborn, consists of a series of stimulating questions under the headings:

Put to other uses?	Substitute?
Adapt?	Rearrange?
Modify?	Reverse?
Magnify?	Combine?
Minify?	

Questions under the heading 'Rearrange', for example, are: Interchange components? Other patterns? Other layout? Other sequence? Transpose cause and effect? Change pace? Change schedule?

The ideal checklist is one you have designed or adapted to use in a particular situation. One simple checklist that is easy to remember, and can be used as a basis for writing your own list of questions, is known by the acronym SCAMPER:

Substitute?	Put to other uses?
Combine?	Eliminate?
Adapt?	Reverse?
Modify?	

Checklists are flexible and can be very useful when you get stuck with a problem. You can also design one consisting of prompts to help you overcome factors which hinder your problem solving (see Chapter 2).

Bug lists

This term is used by James L Adams in his book *Conceptual Blockbusting* to refer to a list of things which cause you, or others, irritation or dissatisfaction. Its purpose is to stimulate the search for opportunities. The method can be applied usefully in organisations by soliciting the opinions of employees in terms of factors such as: What things take you more time than you think is necessary? Why? What situations cause you frustration? Why? What things do you have to do which you think are unnecessary? Why? Answers reveal opportunities for improving job satisfaction as well as improving efficiency.

Analogy

One of the dangers in problem solving is choosing a solution to a current problem because it has worked on a similar (analogous) problem in the past. However, analogies can also provide a model that gives greater insight into a problem. An example of how analogy can lead to innovation is the float technique of glass production. While Alastair Pilkington was washing dishes he noticed the grease floating on the water. When the float technique was perfected it consisted of molten glass floating on a bed of molten tin. Similarly, while at a wine harvest celebration, the German printer Johannes Gutenberg is said to have seen the analogy between the wine press and the concept of printing.

The natural world abounds with analogies that are particularly useful in areas such as engineering and design. You can search for analogies or you may come across one by chance while working on a problem.

Excursions

This term refers to methods used in a group problem-solving technique called Synectics. The purpose is to help distance yourself from a problem to create a fresh perspective. It involves finding metaphors – words or phrases not directly applicable to the problem – which help to suggest solutions. These may have no practical value but they can be made to 'force-fit' the problem, ie forcing them to have some relevance. Here are two examples of excursions:

1. Take an idea from the problem definition and look for examples of it in a totally different environment. For example, if you were looking for ways to reduce the antagonism between members of a team and looked at the world of astronomy:

   ❑ **Gravity pulls planets together** – a grave situation might pull the team together.
   ❑ **The sun 'brightens' the earth** – what might brighten team members?
   ❑ **A dying star disappears in an explosion** – would an 'explosion' clear the air between team members?

2. Look around the room and let your gaze fall upon some object. Then try to relate this to your problem. For example, you've presented a report containing inaccurate information given to you by your deputy and it has lost you an important sale. Your gaze falls on a stapler:

   ❑ 'pin' the blame on your deputy;
   ❑ 'join' forces with your deputy to win back the sale.

This technique is not easy to use but it can bring radical new perspectives to a problem.

Paradoxes

This is another technique used in Synectics. The paradox, also known as a 'book title', is a two-word phrase, usually an adjective and noun, which captures the essence of a problem as a stimulating contradiction. For example, you have a single opportunity to meet two long-standing, valuable clients but at the same time and in different locations. Both meetings are vitally important in their own way. Useful paradoxes might be:

❑ *Attentive neglect*: you will have to neglect one client but want to appear attentive.
❑ *Disloyal allegiance*: you want to avoid appearing disloyal to the client you don't meet.

❏ *Singular double*: you are only one person but need to be two.

Paradoxes, like excursions, help to create new perspectives and suggest new routes to a solution.

Forced relationships

This a simple technique where you deliberately think of combining unrelated objects or ideas to see if there is a new, practical result. There are many commercial products that are the result of such a combination, eg the multipurpose workbench, the Swiss Army knife, talking birthday cards. A more elaborate version of this technique is used in morphological analysis (see below) and similar results can be obtained through attribute listing.

Attribute listing

This is an analytical technique used to identify ways in which a product, service or system could be improved. It consists of three stages:

1. Describe the physical attributes or characteristics of each component of the item.
2. Describe the functions of each component.
3. Examine each component in turn to see if changing its physical attributes would bring about an improvement in its function.

A simple example would be the screwdriver. This has numerous improved variations including a filament for current detection, multiple screw-in shafts, magnetic blades and ratchet mechanisms.

Attribute listing can also be used to search for alternative areas in which a product or service could be used, by looking for applications for individual attributes. The attributes of optical fibres, for instance, have made them useful in fields as diverse as telecommunications, medicine and exhibition lighting.

Another use of attribute listing is in value analysis. This involves looking at the cost of each component of the item in relation to the function it performs. Components that are disproportionately costly in relation to their function may be eliminated or ways found to reduce their cost. The aim is to increase the ratio of value to cost.

A fourth application is in analysing systems to find areas of potential improvement. For example, the attributes of a waste product may be analysed to search for ways in which it could be used as a raw material for another product or a new product. Ideally this would also use parts of the existing production system.

Morphological analysis

This term refers to a variety of techniques which are similar to forced relationships and attribute listing. They can be applied to ideas, problems, objects or systems that are broken down into their individual components so that every possible combination can be searched for something new and practical.

Although there are several variations, a simple method involves the following stages:

❑   list the parameters of the situation;
❑   subdivide each into its smallest parts;
❑   represent these parts in a matrix;
❑   examine all possible combinations of these parts.

There are a variety of ways to represent this information. Cards or sheets of paper can be used to list each component, either individually or grouped under headings, and then shuffled to create various combinations. Alternatively the information can be grouped and written on the outer edge of different sized circles of card, which are pinned together through the centre and rotated to bring different components together. Perhaps the easiest method is to draw a three-dimensional cube divided into many smaller cubes, as in Figure 6.1 This simple example is based on using incentives to reward managers for specific behaviour at work, either on a regular basis, on merit, or at the

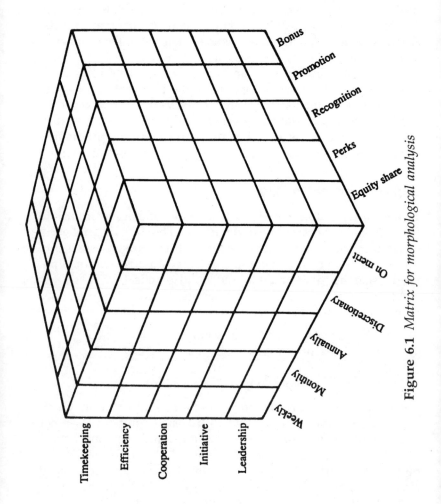

Figure 6.1 *Matrix for morphological analysis*

discretion of someone more senior. It uses only three sides of the cube, giving 125 possible combinations, but it illustrates how ideas can be brought together in different ways, eg giving recognition for good timekeeping on a weekly basis, discretionary bonuses for showing initiative, promotion on merit for leadership qualities, or awarding points towards an equity share in the company based on efficiency during the past year.

The main use of morphological analysis is in the development of new products, services and systems, eg analysing the components of current successful products to find new combinations of attractive features. It has been successful particularly in the area of new technologies. Although it's time-consuming it forces a thorough search of all possible combinations which would not be realistic unaided.

A more sophisticated version of morphological analysis is known by the acronym SCIMITAR (Systematic Creativity and Integrative Modelling for Industrial Technology And Research), which was developed in the chemical industry by John Carson. The axes of the cubic model are used to represent, for example, the materials, processes and markets of a company. Existing products are assigned one of the smaller cubes in the model, according to the materials, processes and markets involved. Then each unoccupied cube is examined to see what product would result from the combination of material and process, and which market it could serve. Considering other materials, processes and markets can be used to identify new business opportunities.

The best idea-generation technique to use is often determined by the type of problem and your goal. In situations where you have a choice, practice will tell you which ones work best for you. Although some of the techniques may appear cumbersome and time-consuming, with practice you will find they become less mechanical.

7

SOLVING PROBLEMS IN A GROUP

A lot of problem solving takes place in group settings. Meetings and informal discussions, for example, are often used to air different ideas and points of view to help solve problems for which participants have either shared respons- ibility or a contribution to make. Most of the time, however, we don't take full advantage of group settings. It can be the best way to solve some problems but only if it is used properly.

WHEN TO USE GROUP PROBLEM SOLVING

There are definite advantages in using a group to solve certain problems, but others can be solved more effectively by an individual. It is important to know when and when not to work in a group. The following checklist can help you decide.

❏ Can the problem be defined in many different ways?
❏ Is information from many different sources required?
❏ Is it a specialised problem, where the 'expert' might be biased or not see the wider implications?
❏ Does the problem have implications for many people?
❏ Are there likely to be many possible solutions?

❏ Is it a complex problem with many different aspects?

❏ Will a solution need to be agreed by others before it can be implemented?

The more questions to which you answer 'yes', the more appropriate it is to use group problem solving. However, the deciding question is always: 'Are suitable and relevant people available to work together in solving this problem?'

GETTING THE BEST OUT OF GROUP PROBLEM SOLVING

Problem solving is a complex and at times frustrating process. It requires a careful manipulation of mental skills, which is very susceptible to outside influence. When people are working together it is inevitable that they will influence each other. This can have a significant effect on the efficiency of group problem solving. To get the best results the situation must be carefully managed to minimise the possible adverse effects and maximise the benefits. The benefits and potential drawbacks are summarised in Table 7.1.

Potential drawbacks

People working in a group sometimes perceive the situation as competitive. This generates behaviour that is destructive and drains the creative energy of the group. For example, if someone disagrees with our ideas we can perceive it as a put-down. The automatic reaction may be to disagree with that person's ideas when an opportunity arises. It seems to bolster our self-esteem. We may also totally ignore what others are suggesting in our eagerness to express our own ideas. Power-seekers may use ploys such as highlighting flaws in others' arguments and displays of expertise to show their supremacy. These types of behaviour create an atmosphere that is incompatible with effective problem solving.

Table 7.1 *Benefits and potential drawbacks of group problem solving*

BENEFITS	POTENTIAL DRAWBACKS
Greater output	Competition
Cross-fertilisation	Conformity
Reduced bias	Lack of objective direction
Increased risk taking	Time constraints
Higher commitment	
Improved communication	
Better solutions	

Another drawback is the strong tendency for individuals in a group to want to conform to the consensus. This can be for a variety of reasons, including the need to feel liked, valued or respected, and it tends to make people censor their ideas accordingly. The comparative 'status' of the individuals present also has an important influence. Senior members often want to maintain their image of being knowledgeable, while junior members want to avoid appearing the inexperienced 'upstart'. Because agreement on ideas can be gained quickly in a group setting, groups also tend to select and approve solutions quickly without exploring all the possibilities.

Most traditional meetings and group discussions convened to solve problems are ineffectively directed. Sometimes there is no effective leader to give direction to the discussion, with the result that it wanders aimlessly. When there is strong leadership the group leader or chairperson often exerts undue pressure on the direction and content of the discussion. In addition, the ideas aired during a meeting are not usually recorded, apart from the minutes and individual note-taking. The result is that many ideas are forgotten and don't serve as a constant stimulus to the discussion.

Time constraints are another drawback. Group problem solving is a relatively slow process compared with working alone. It requires individuals to come together at an agreed time, perhaps for an hour. This can cause organisational problems as well as impatience amongst participants to 'get it over with' as quickly as possible.

Benefits

A major advantage of group problem solving is that it can generate a lot of ideas. Simply because of the number of people involved, each with differing experience, knowledge, points of view and values, a larger number and variety of ideas for solutions can be produced. Cross-fertilisation is also valuable. The exchange of ideas can act as a stimulus to the imagination, encouraging individuals to explore ideas they would not otherwise have considered.

The shared responsibility of a group in arriving at decisions can encourage individuals to explore seemingly unrealistic ideas and to challenge accepted ways of doing things. Individual biases and prejudices can be challenged by the group, forcing the individual to recognise them. Group pressure can also encourage individuals to accept that change is needed. Shared responsibility makes individuals more willing to take risks. The discussion of different points of view also helps the group to be more realistic in assessing the risks associated with particular courses of action.

Working as a group can also result in more commitment to ideas. When goals are agreed it gives a common purpose to the group, within which individuals can gain a feeling of self-determination and recognition through their contribution. Individuals who have contributed to finding a solution feel a greater commitment to its successful implementation.

Communication is obviously improved among particip-ants and this also has a beneficial effect. When people who are affected by a problem or who will be involved in implementa-tion are involved in finding a solution, they will know how and why that particular solution was chosen. Also, people with knowledge relevant to the problem can communicate that knowledge directly if they participate in solving the problem.

Maximising the benefits

Properly managed, and used in the right situations, group problem solving results in better solutions. Groups can bring a broader range of ideas, knowledge and skills to bear on a problem. This creates a stimulating interaction of diverse ideas which results in a wider range and better quality of solutions.

Various methods have been developed to capitalise on the strengths of group problem solving and to overcome its potential weaknesses. These specify the role of the participants, including the leader, and the methods used by the group.

Participants should be selected to give the group a diversity of experience in various disciplines. Not all should be familiar with the problem area. People with little or no relevant experience bring a new perspective and are more likely to think of unusual solutions. All participants should understand the function of the group and what is expected of them. A mix of men and women, of quiet and lively personalities and of ages creates a stimulating interaction. The mixing of widely differing 'ranks' should be avoided, especially in organisations where employees are conscious of status. Some people are reticent to suggest unusual ideas in front of others of higher or lower rank (see page 22).

The methods used, which are described later in this chapter, are designed to stimulate creativity and give coherent direction to individual contributions. They help relieve the pressures and constraints of a normal meeting and create an atmosphere and frame of mind conducive to creative problem solving. The group leader plays a key role in generating the right kind of atmosphere and prompting individuals in their search for solutions.

Leadership of group problem solving is different to the traditional role of chairing a meeting. The chair normally decides the issues to be discussed and judges the relevant comments and areas worthy of exploration. The leader in group problem solving is there primarily to stimulate and record ideas from other participants. The precise role varies slightly in different group techniques but basically it includes:

❑ Briefing participants.
❑ Keeping contributions flowing at a fast pace.
❑ Ensuring everyone contributes.
❑ Clarifying ideas when necessary.
❑ Ensuring everyone sticks to the 'rules'.
❑ Not allowing anyone to be put on the defensive.
❑ Prompting individuals to build on each other's ideas.
❑ Prompting the group to explore new avenues.
❑ Ensuring quiet and less experienced individuals are given a chance to air their ideas.
❑ Recording and displaying the group's ideas.

The primary function of the leader is not to allow any participant to be put on the defensive. They must be free to concentrate on thinking up ideas rather than defending them. During idea generation anyone who judges or criticises ideas – through words, tone or gesture – is told forcefully by the leader to 'suspend judgement'. The purpose is to avoid excluding impractical or seemingly ridiculous ideas which later could be developed into something useful. A good knowledge of the mechanics of the particular technique, an infectious enthusiasm and a good sense of humour are ideal characteristics for the leader.

TECHNIQUES

Brainstorming is the most popular technique designed specifically for group problem solving. Quality circles, described later, are primarily concerned with problem solving but serve additional, broader functions.

Brainstorming

Brainstorming, which was devised in an advertising agency, is designed to generate a large number and range of ideas in a short time. This is achieved by concentrating solely on idea generation and creating a light-hearted, free-wheeling atmosphere.

The number of people in a brainstorming session varies between 5 and 20, with an optimum of about 12. Everyone present contributes ideas, including the leader, because non-participating observers can have an inhibiting effect. Sessions are held in a room away from distractions, with chairs arranged in a U-shape and a flipchart for recording ideas. Each sheet of paper is torn off once full and pinned to a wall clearly visible to the participants. Sessions can last anything up to two hours, although the longer the session the more difficult it is to sustain the flow of ideas. The finishing time should be left open so that it doesn't curtail a fruitful session.

The leader's role begins with preparation for the session. This involves gaining a full understanding of the problem, selecting and inviting participants and giving them a brief description of the problem. During the session the leader stimulates, contributes and records ideas. Constant structured stimulation by the leader is needed to keep everyone participating and the ideas flowing. It is the leader's job to enforce the four basic rules of a brainstorming session:

1. *Suspend judgement*. No evaluation is allowed during the session and the leader must be able to enforce this rule even with very senior colleagues.

2. *Free-wheel*. This is the lowering of barriers and inhibitions about what is practical and impractical so that the mind can wander freely. It is encouraged by the 'suspend judgement' rule and by humour and laughter in response to silly ideas.

3. *Cross-fertilise*. Participants are encouraged to modify and develop other people's ideas and to express any other ideas these suggest.

4. *Quantity is good*. Participants are encouraged to produce a large number of ideas irrespective of whether they are practical or impractical. A good session can produce hundreds of ideas.

All energy in a brainstorming session is directed towards producing ideas for solving the problem. There is no evaluation of ideas. The session consists of four stages: defining and discussing the problem, restating the problem, warming up, and brainstorming.

1. *Defining and discussing the problem*. The problem is described briefly by someone with knowledge of the situation, giving sufficient information for the others to understand it but not enough to inhibit their ideas for a solution. This stage usually takes around five minutes.

2. *Restating the problem*. Group members restate the problem, looking at it from different angles and phrasing it in terms of 'How to ...?' The leader writes these down. Throughout the session all ideas are numbered serially to make them easier to identify later. Restatement continues until all ideas are exhausted. This should result in at least 25 restatements, often many more.

3. *Warming up*. At this stage it's useful to use a fluency exercise, eg 'other uses for ...' and the consequences of bizarre situations (see page 68). This helps get participants in a free-wheeling frame of mind. None of these ideas are recorded.

4. *Brainstorming*. One of the restatements is selected either by the leader or by voting. The leader writes this down on a new sheet of paper, rephrased as: 'In how many ways can we ...?' The leader reads the restatement aloud and asks for ideas, writing them down as they are called out. When a sheet is full it

is displayed prominently on the wall to act as a stimulus to further ideas. When all ideas have been exhausted another restatement is selected, as remote as possible from the first, and the process repeated. Three or four restatements are treated in this way.

There are various things the leader can do to stimulate the group, including repeating ideas as they are written down, asking for variations on an earlier idea, calling for another warming up exercise, and using the following types of non-limiting prompt:

- ❏ Tell me ways in which we could achieve that.
- ❏ Any ideas?
- ❏ Can we build on this?
- ❏ Can we do that in a different way?
- ❏ What would be the ideal?
- ❏ Let's have some really wild ideas.
- ❏ Who cares – let's just play with the idea.
- ❏ Can you tell me more about that?

When ideas dry up the leader asks the group to select the wildest idea from the lists and suggest useful variations. A couple of the wildest ideas are treated in this way before the leader ends the session with a description of the evaluation process.

Evaluation takes place another day, once a list of all the ideas produced has been compiled. There are two methods of evaluation – by a small team of people selected from the original session, including the leader and others committed to solving the problem, and by all the participants individually. Using both methods helps to prevent potentially useful ideas being discarded.

The list of ideas is sent to participants who are each asked to select a small proportion of ideas they feel could be useful. They send the numbers of these ideas to the leader, who collates them and discards ideas that received few votes. The team of selected individuals also meets to discuss the full list of ideas. They use criteria of effectiveness to weed out the impractical ideas and then select the best ones. The two lists of remaining ideas are collated by the leader and the highest voting ideas selected for further evaluation. At this stage the ideas are examined to see how they could be modified and improved before they are rejected or accepted. Various creative techniques described in Chapter 6 can be used for this purpose.

Under some circumstances brainstorming sessions can be conducted successfully in a less structured way. One particular application is in the creation of brand names. Starting with a product description, and under the direction of a leader, group members explore all the associations a product might trigger in the mind of the consumer. Visual images of the various lifestyles associated with the product can be used to help stimulate ideas for names. A two-hour session, with several products under consideration, may generate around 2000 names. Later these are screened carefully. Names already in use are thrown out together with those which in foreign translation would have negative associations.

Quality circles

Quality circles have a broader function than brainstorming and therefore are not so narrowly structured and controlled. They are intended as a way of using problem solving to improve the quality of the company's products and reduce costs. They also deliver other benefits including increased staff awareness of quality, greater job satisfaction, improved motivation and better communications.

Quality circles consist of around 4 to 12 people from the same work area who meet voluntarily on a regular basis to solve their work-related problems. Typically meetings are held weekly, fortnightly or monthly and range in length from one to two hours. They are held in paid time and a room is usually set aside for the sole use of the circle. It is equipped with noticeboards, flipcharts, presentation and computer facilities, etc. The circle leader is often the supervisor of the work group involved and usually has been on a short off-the-job training course to learn about the method and the leader's role. Circle members contribute ideas on problem areas to be tackled and invite suggestions from others outside the group, voting to decide which problem they will tackle first.

Information needed to solve the problem is collected by the group, including management information relating to the problem, eg the cost of an existing process or the manufacturing costs of a product. Various creative techniques are used to suggest a range of possible solutions, including brainstorming and force-field analysis. The circle evaluates solutions in terms of their effectiveness, their effects on other departments, the costs and savings to the company, and the likelihood of their acceptance by management.

When a solution has been selected it is presented at a meeting with the relevant management. This presentation is often rehearsed and includes a description of the problem, an explanation of why it was considered a problem, the recommended solution and its benefits, and an outline of the action required for implementation. When practical, circle members are also involved in implementation of the solution. Usually there is no financial reward for ideas, although in some companies the ideas can be put into a suggestion scheme which may result in payment.

Communication between members of the quality circle and the rest of the workforce is extremely important. As well as inviting ideas on problems to be tackled, the circle reports regularly to employees on its activities. Maintaining a high visibility for the circle is important in meeting many of its objectives.

Setting up and running a quality circle programme requires planning and management. A management committee, usually consisting of representatives of various rank from different departments, initiates the programme. It also makes decisions on its development, the methods for selecting leaders and members, how circles will operate and the evaluation policy. A facilitator or coordinator deals with the day-to-day running of the circles.

Not everyone has access to properly run group problem-solving sessions. However, we can all appreciate the need sometimes to get the wider perspective afforded by a collaborative effort. If you are aware of the potential pitfalls you can gain some of the benefits of group problem solving through well-managed meetings. It doesn't offer the same group dynamic for idea generation and cross-fertilisation, but you can benefit from shared experience and knowledge. If the problem affects you all you can also share the responsibility for solving it!

EVALUATING SOLUTIONS

When you have more than one possible solution, each with a different mix of advantages and disadvantages, you need to evaluate them to identify the most effective. Even with only one solution you must decide if it is acceptable and, if so, take the decision to implement it.

Identifying which solution will be most effective in achieving your objective is a complex decision-making process. It requires a methodical evaluation of all the options against the exact requirements of your ideal solution. Even then your selection will often be a compromise between conflicting needs and between the benefits and drawbacks of each solution. It is easy to make the wrong choice. Some of the main reasons are:

❑ Not being methodical.
❑ Not considering all the alternatives.
❑ Not using appropriate evaluation techniques.
❑ Inaccurate forecasting of the effects of different actions and external influences.
❑ Uncritical acceptance of subjective judgements.

Once we have made a decision we are often reluctant to change our mind even when we know we have not made the best choice. It is easier to ensure you make the right decision first time.

WHO SHOULD BE INVOLVED IN EVALUATION?

There are many situations where we can choose a solution, and implement it, without involving anyone else in the decision-making process. Sometimes you might consult others out of personal regard for them or because it's politic. At other times it may be essential. Examples are when you have a formal obligation to consult others and when you need information, skills, knowledge or commitment from other people.

You may have to consult others because of the type of decisions you will be making, eg if they involve actions beyond your authority. For effective evaluation you may need additional information, eg about what would be a satisfactory solution, what value should be placed on different outcomes, or what resources are available to implement a solution. Evaluation might also require expertise in particular areas, eg predicting the consequences of new tax legislation, analysis of an overseas market, or forecasting the reaction of staff to a new working practice.

Gaining the commitment of others may be integral to solving a problem effectively. People affected can include those who have to agree the solution, 'live with it', implement it or provide the necessary resources. At work this may not be restricted to company employees but could include customers or suppliers, for example.

A good way of gaining commitment is to involve people in the decision-making process, although this can have drawbacks. In particular, the decision-making process can become more complicated and protracted. Be sure that you need their commitment and that involving them is the best or only way. Ask yourself: Why do I need their commitment? Do those I need to involve have a common view of the purpose of this decision? If not, there could be conflicting interests at work and it may be better to look for another way of encouraging their commitment. Could you gain their commitment without involving them in decision making, eg offer them persuasive benefits, use your authority?

You can involve other people either individually or collectively. When you work with others on a one-to-one basis usually you retain overall responsibility for the decision. In a group you can either retain the option to veto the group's decision or take part as an equal member and agree to accept the collective decision. Group decision making has the advantage that responsibility is shared and individual subjective bias or prejudice is reduced.

EVALUATING SOLUTIONS

There are different ways to evaluate solutions. Basically it involves identifying and comparing their relative values, which are recorded and presented in a meaningful way to aid comparison. This information can also be useful in persuading others to accept the decision and communicating the solution to those implementing it.

Sometimes our decision making is influenced to varying extents by subjective values. For example, we can reasonably rely on personal preferences when choosing a holiday destination; and we rely heavily on past experience and our intuition when we must make a snap decision. However, we are so accustomed to using our own values in decision making that they can mislead us when an objective decision is required. The opinions and preferences of those involved in a problem situation must be considered, but only as part of the objective evaluation of the options.

The evaluation process can be divided into five stages:

1. Defining the 'ideal' solution.
2. Eliminating unviable solutions, ie those which do not meet the constraints.
3. Evaluating the remaining solutions against the results required.
4. Assessing the risks associated with the 'best' solution.
5. Taking the decision.

Defining the ideal solution

The criteria of effectiveness defined for a solution (see page 59) are inadequate to make an effective evaluation. Each solution may differ slightly or radically in the way and the extent to which it achieves your various goals. To evaluate these effectively you need to construct a model of the 'ideal' solution against which to measure them. Consider the outcomes required and the constraints that have to be met.

Outcomes

Outcomes include the benefits required in terms of the objective as well as dealing effectively with obstacles or causes and sometimes gaining acceptance of the solution (and/or its effects) by other people. Depending on your objective, the benefits desired may be fixed (eg restarting a halted production line) or flexible (eg achieving the highest possible market share).

Achieving the desired results means that you must have dealt effectively with obstacles or causes so you can omit these from your list of results required. If, for example, you increased productivity by 8 per cent by reallocating work it means you will have overcome possible resistance from those affected. Other situations may not be so clear-cut. Then you need to define what it means to deal effectively with obstacles or causes. To achieve and maintain world-class customer service, for example, you would need to continually monitor customer perceptions of service. This could involve overcoming barriers to communication between them and the company.

When acceptance of the solution by others is essential you need to list the factors that will make it acceptable to them, eg not increasing their workload, not introducing monotonous tasks.

Constraints

Constraints are generally specified as the limits of resources (time, space, money, materials, people), the minimum results acceptable and the maximum disadvantages that can be tolerated.

Table 8.1 *Example of an 'ideal' solution*

PROBLEM
Reduce expenditure on stationery from £1850 per month to under £1500 per month within 4 months.

RESULTS REQUIRED
Expenditure on stationery under £1500 per month (a 19% reduction)
Wastage, misuse and pilfering of stationery prevented
A simple administrative system

CONSTRAINTS
Target to be achieved within 4 months
No additional administrative time beyond the current level, once the target has been achieved
Supplier cannot be changed (for political reasons)
A 12% reduction in costs would be acceptable initially
A blatant 'policing' strategy will not be acceptable

Resources may be limited by what is available or what the problem justifies. Minimum acceptable results may be stated in absolute terms (eg achieving 100 per cent accuracy in quality control) or relative terms (eg achieving 100 per cent accuracy provided it does not cost over £18,000 per annum). The maximum tolerable disadvantages are stated in terms of unacceptable cost in resources and undesirable side-effects.

Other factors may also represent a constraint, eg company policy (perhaps dictating how certain issues are handled) and legislation (such as local planning restrictions). A simple example of how an ideal solution might be defined in shown in Table 8.1. There would be many different ways of achieving this ideal solution, each providing different benefits and drawbacks. One solution, for example, might achieve a saving by distributing stationery regularly on a controlled basis, but run the risk of sometimes leaving people without essential items. Another solution might be to make people accountable for their station-ery costs, but this could be viewed as petty and involve extra paperwork, putting an additional burden on already over-worked staff.

It is often difficult to choose between solutions which have different disadvantages and which provide the results required in different amounts. For example, would it be better to prevent wastage of stationery completely even if it required complex administration, or to accept reduced wastage using a simpler system? To deal with this type of situation you need to give points to each result required according to its relative value. This is done by selecting the most important result, giving it an arbitrary value (eg 5) and then rating all the other results against this standard. In the earlier example, simplicity of administra-tion might be given a value of 5 while reduction in expenditure is rated 4. Disadvantages are given negative values according to their relative severity. Deciding the relative values of results and disadvantages can be difficult and it may require discussion with others to ensure the values are objective.

Decisions are not always made by choosing the optimum mix of all the criteria of effectiveness. Instead the following strate-gies may be used in certain situations:

1. Selecting any solution which achieves a minimum set of requirements. This strategy could be used when there is insufficient time or information for a detailed or full evalua-tion.

2. Giving preference to one particular evaluation criterion, eg employ the person with the best telephone manner. This might be used when one criterion has particular significance and there is insufficient time or information for a full evaluation.

3. Giving preference to solutions with minimal disadvantage on a particular criterion, eg buy the make of popular car that shows minimum depreciation.

You can check your ideal solution by answering the following questions:

❏ Is it an accurate reflection of what would be ideal under the circumstances?

✎
_____

_____

_____

_____

❏ Does it take account of the needs of all the people involved?

✎
_____

_____

_____

_____

❏ Are any conflicting or inconsistent results desired?

✎
_____

_____

_____

_____

❏ Are the relative values given to the criteria of effectiveness free from bias or other distortions?

✎
_____

_____

❏ Do the values conform to departmental and organisational policies?

✎

_____

_____

_____

_____

When the outcome of a particular course of action is uncertain you need to estimate the probabilities of what will happen. In trying to find 80 new dealers to stock a company product, for example, you may have considered, among other approaches, direct mail and personal visits by sales staff. To evaluate these two courses of action you would need to estimate the conversion rate for each, ie the probability of a new dealer being recruited per visit and per mail piece. Probability is expressed as a figure between 0 and 1, where 0 is no probability and 1 is complete certainty. The probability of finding a new dealer through a mail shot, for example, may be 0.01 (1 per cent conversion, or one new dealer for each 100 mailed) and through a personal visit, 0.14 (14 per cent conversion, or 14 new dealers per 100 visits). Probabilities must also be calculated where costs and side-effects are uncertain.

You are now ready to begin evaluating solutions. The method described below reduces the time required for evaluation by first eliminating solutions that do not meet the constraints.

Eliminating unviable solutions

At this stage you examine each solution in turn and reject those which do not meet all the constraints you have identified.

Record the reasons so that you can check them later. Sometimes it is possible to modify an otherwise unacceptable solution so that it comes within the constraints and can be evaluated further.

Evaluating the remaining solutions

Each of the remaining solutions is examined to see how well it provides the results required. The best fit on each dimension of the results is given an arbitrary value (eg 5) and the others are valued relative to this standard. As each solution is evaluated the results can be recorded in a table. The simple example in Table 8.2 shows how solutions can be rated against results required. The value of each solution in relation to desired results is found by multiplying its fit against the relative value of each result (bracketed). Disadvantages of each solution are rated independently and given a negative value. The 'best' solution is the one with the highest aggregate score.

The fictional example in Table 8.2 concerns ways to reverse the fall in trade of a family-owned restaurant. Redecoration and press advertising have been rejected because of cost constraints. Each solution is composed of a variety of strategies. Improving the food, for example, may involve changing the chef, improving the quality of produce used or improving kitchen facilities, depending on the existing situation. These are not shown but normally they would all be included, rated against the results required, along with the disadvantages. The probability of different outcomes may also be important, eg the likely response rate to mailshots.

In this example, improving the service is most likely to reverse the fall in trade, followed closely by improving the food. The two solutions in combination may exceed the results required but may also exceed constraints, eg the combined costs of better produce and retraining staff.

Before moving to the next stage check your evaluation to ensure it is accurate and you have not omitted any relevant factors.

Table 8.2 *Rating solutions against results required*

POSSIBLE SOLUTIONS	RESULTS REQUIRED							DISADVANT-AGES (−)		OVERALL VALUE
	Regain lost customers (4)		Attract new customers (4)		Create regular customer base (5)					
Improve food	5	20	4	16	5	25	Cost of better produce	− 3		58
Improve service	5	20	5	20	5	25	Retrain staff	− 1		64
Change menu regularly	3	12	5	20	4	20	Careful planning required	− 1		51
Extend opening hours	3	12	4	16	4	20	Increased overheads	− 3		45
Create mailing list	2	8	0	0	5	25	Cost vs. Response	− 1		32

Assessing risks

The solution chosen by this stage offers the best balance of benefits versus disadvantages. Now you need to examine the possible risks associated with this solution. Are they acceptable and could they be minimised?

To assess risks associated with each solution you need to answer the question, 'What could go wrong, how likely is it to happen and how severe would the effects be?' Risks are most likely to arise from using inaccurate information during development and evaluation of solutions, and during implementation.

To review the likely risks associated with inaccurate information ask yourself:

❏ Is there information that was key to the construction or evaluation of this solution?

❏ Is this information reliable? (Think about the source, eg it could be biased – and the method of collection.)

❏ Have any assumptions been made?

❏ Are there any areas where we have no experience or knowledge of the likely outcome?

If you suspect any of the information used is unreliable you should double-check. If your suspicions are confirmed you must decide what implications it has for the likely success of the solution. For example, a company might have estimated that productivity would increase 15 per cent by installing new machinery. A review of the figures shows this to be nearer 8 per cent. Is the purchase still viable given the reduced productivity gain?

A solution can also become unreliable during implementation. You need to consider what could happen if the implementation of a solution does not go as planned. For example:

❏ Is there sufficient leeway in meeting constraints and the results required? If it takes 5 per cent extra time to implement this solution will we still meet the deadline? If there is a price increase in this raw material will we exceed our budget?
❏ Are the resources required of such magnitude or extend over such a prolonged period that it will leave us vulnerable? If profits over the next eight months are committed to this expansion programme what will happen if someone launches a competitive service, our market share falls dramatically and profits are reduced?

❏   If we do not keep to this time schedule could it mean that resources required at some stage of implementation will not be available, eg because we move into a new financial year or because they are required elsewhere?

❏   Does the effectiveness of this solution rely upon the actions of other people and:
  – are they capable of carrying out what is required?
  – are they likely to meet our expectations?
  – are there any personal or political reasons why they may not behave as expected and required?

❏   Could external factors throw us off course or prevent us carrying out certain parts of our plan, eg national disputes or changes in social attitudes, legislation, the environment or the economy?

Sometimes it is necessary to draw up a rough plan for implementation before you can determine the potential risks, eg in terms of keeping to the time schedule. Planning for implementation is described in Chapter 10 (page 119).

When you have identified areas of risk you need to calculate the probability of an undesirable outcome and the severity of its effects. For example, there is a probability of 0.25 (25 per cent chance) that our major competitor is nearer than us to launching this new service. If this happens it means our intention of being first in the market will fail and our 'solution' will be costly.

Some types of situation inevitably carry a substantial amount of risk, eg developing new technologies. If possible you should build into your solution ways of minimising risks, although ultimately you need to identify an acceptable level of risk for each risk factor.

If the risks associated with a particular solution are found to be unacceptable and inescapable it must be rejected and the next highest scoring solution evaluated for risks. This process continues until a fully acceptable solution is found.

Taking the decision

When you take a decision you commit yourself to a particular course of action and take responsibility for its consequences. If you do not make the commitment and take the decision the problem will remain unsolved. Being methodical and thorough in evaluating solutions adds to your confidence in taking this vital step.

Once you have chosen a viable solution you may need approval to implement it. Even when this is not essential it is wise to seek the approval of the people affected and those who will be involved in implementation. Chapter 9 examines how to present your solution to them in the most effective way.

9

GETTING A SOLUTION ACCEPTED

Once you have decided on a solution you may need other people's cooperation, approval or authority to implement it. With routine problems, where there is common understanding of what is involved, often this is straightforward. You simply notify the relevant people of your decision and how it will affect them. With complex and uncommon problems, however, and where major change or extensive use of resources is required, you must present your solution in detail. To do this effectively you need to understand the reasons people may oppose and possibly reject your solution, prepare a presentation that encourages their acceptance, and deliver the presentation effectively.

Situations in which you need to 'sell' your solution to other people are examined in Chapter 8 (see page 92). If you have involved these people in finding and evaluating solutions you may already have gained their approval and commitment. However, it will still be necessary to let them have details of your implementation plan (see page 119), which forms part of your presentation of the solution for approval.

REASONS FOR OPPOSITION

CASE STUDY

The manager of a small research and development team in the packaging industry decided the team would work more effectively if she coordinated individuals' efforts more closely. Unbeknown to the group, she spent three weeks devising a new management plan. It stated that the team would no longer tackle problems by pooling their intellectual resources. Instead she would write individuals a detailed brief on what areas she would like each of them to explore. No detailed reasons for the change were given. Ten minutes before the end of work on a Friday afternoon she called the team together. Handing out copies of her plan, she said: 'I've decided we can do a better job if individually you concentrate on different aspects of each project. Read this over the weekend and give me your reaction on Monday.'

Irrespective of whether this manager's plan was a good idea or not, she made some serious errors:

❑ It was likely to involve a change in working methods so she should have involved team members in looking for solutions.

❑ The plan mentioned nothing about her reasons for believing there was a problem, or how the new method of working would be more effective.

❑ She presented her 'solution' at the end of the working week; this robbed individuals of the opportunity to discuss their concerns, which were likely to fester and create resentment before Monday arrived.

❑ Her manner of introducing the plan suggested a *fait accompli*.

However good a solution, the way it is presented to people involved or affected can determine whether it will succeed or fail. The more opposition there is to your proposal the more likely it is to be rejected. Even if the people with the power to sanction the proposal are not opposed to it, opposition from others may influence their decision. It is therefore vital to identify potential areas of major opposition so that you can plan how to overcome them.

There are many reasons people may oppose a solution presented to them. Some of the key reasons are described below.

Not all of these are related directly to the ideas and actions concerned.

A poor solution. Any solution which does not deal with the problem effectively, or is impractical, or does not take into consideration all the relevant factors should be opposed. If the solution does not fit the problem, or has unacceptable side-effects, you should not propose it.

Nature of the problem. The more serious the consequences for those considering your proposal the more closely they will scrutinise it. If the people involved have a good knowledge of the problem, or aspects of the solution, they will also scrutinise it closely. Any aspects of your solution which do not conform to their ideas or expectations may be opposed simply because of differences of opinion.

Lack of interest in the problem can create opposition when people feel you are wasting their time by involving them. Lack of knowledge of the problem area can also create opposition if you do not give people sufficient information for them to understand your reasoning.

Individual needs and expectations of those involved will colour their perceptions of, and reaction to, your proposal. An individual who has a strong need to feel independent, for example, may oppose any solution that increases collective responsibility or encourages group working. Expectations of the outcome of solving a problem can also create opposition. For example, someone with a grievance against the current method of grading because it gives more value to qualifications than performance may oppose any grading system that does not value performance highly.

Resistance to change. Some people and some organisations are strongly resistant to change. A solution that involves considerable change in the *status quo* may therefore meet strong opposition even when it is good and well presented. Some organisations do not have the structure or resources to accommodate major change and so senior management are likely to veto such solutions.

Mistrust of the solution. Many people have an in-built suspicion of solutions that are highly innovative, or yield high rewards by a simple method that seems 'too good to be true'.

Poor presentation. You can create opposition by not presenting your solution effectively, eg not demonstrating that the benefits outweigh the disadvantages, not showing that you have considered side-effects and risks, not giving adequate information or communicating it effectively (so people either misunderstand or cannot recognise the value of the solution).

Poor timing. However sound the basic idea, an ill-timed solution can meet with opposition, eg proposing a solution that requires permanent additional manpower shortly after redundancies in another department, suggesting a more centralised management structure when current policy is to promote greater autonomy of company divisions.

Unsolicited ideas. If you have taken it upon yourself to solve a particular problem, or exploit an opportunity, and have not mentioned this to people involved or affected, your solution will come as a complete surprise. It could be received in a number of ways. They may be interested without having any intention of adopting your ideas. They may feel that you are interfering and perhaps even criticising them for the way they currently do things. They may refuse to listen to your idea. All of these responses are legitimate under the circumstances.

It is a waste of your time, and could create antagonism, if you try to force ideas upon others. The only time it is worth presenting an unsolicited solution to people is when they have answered yes to a question like, 'I think I have found a way to . . ., would you be interested in hearing more?'

Interpersonal conflict. Your relationship with those you are presenting to, and their perceptions of you, can have a profound effect on their reaction. These factors are complex and may have developed over long periods. A young and enthusiastic manager who is keen on applying the latest techniques, for example, may meet opposition from a more mature, traditional manager who resents the attempt at change. Similarly, at some time in the distant past you may have criticised or rejected someone's ideas. When it is time to listen to your ideas that person may still feel resentment.

Getting a good solution accepted (don't ever try to sell a bad solution!) is a matter of persuasive communication. Preparation is the key to success.

WHY MAY PEOPLE OPPOSE YOUR SOLUTION?

To identify why your proposal may be opposed you must analyse the problem, its solution and the people involved and affected. Once you know the likely reasons for opposition you can include counters to these objections in your presentation. The first step is to list the attributes of the problem and your solution that affect other people. Ask yourself questions such as:

❏ Who does the problem affect?

_____

_____

_____

_____

❏ What adverse effects are they experiencing?

_____

_____

_____

_____

❏ Which of these adverse effects does the solution remove?

❏ Does the solution call for major changes and who will be affected most?

❏ Does the solution have adverse side-effects and for whom?

❏ Is the solution unusual and in what ways?

❑ Does its implementation require exceptional cooperation or action by any individuals and how?

✎

This type of questioning will help you identify aspects of the solution that are likely to be of most interest to your audience. Some areas of possible opposition may be apparent already, eg if your solution does not deal with all the adverse effects of the problem. To complete the list ask yourself, 'How are people likely to react to this solution?' Use questions such as:

❑ Do any aspects of the problem or its solution have special significance for them? Does it reflect badly on their previous performance or judgement? Does it infringe on their area of operation or detract from their authority? Does it compete with their needs for resources?
❑ In what way will they want the situation to change when the problem is solved? Does the solution achieve this?
❑ Will they gain or lose with this solution? How and by how much?
❑ Will they want to achieve or gain something for themselves or others through this solution?
❑ Do they hold particularly strong views on any aspect of the problem or its solution? Do they have an axe to grind?
❑ Do they have stereotyped views, eg favouring the traditional approach?

You are also one of the people involved, so you need to consider additional factors such as:

❑ What is their personal opinion of me, eg do any of them have reason to resent or mistrust me?
❑ Are our views of the situation likely to coincide or differ, by how much, and in what ways?

By comparing your answers to all these questions you can identify the major sources of opposition. Assuming that your solution is timely, sound and deals with the problem effectively, all these potential causes of opposition can be avoided or countered in the way you present your solution.

PLANNING YOUR PRESENTATION

Depending on the situation you may present your solution verbally or in a written report. If you have a choice, a meeting gives you the opportunity to get immediate feedback and respond persuasively to doubts and objections. A report, on the other hand, gives you more control over the words you use and the effects they have. Most solutions that involve major changes or extensive use of resources are presented in reports.

Persuading people to accept your solution means giving them reason to accept it rather than oppose it. Some of the ways to achieve this are described below.

Anticipate opposition. From analysing the problem, your solution and your audience, you should have a good idea of the opposition that could arise. Prepare responses to questions and objections that are likely to be raised. It is important to explain the disadvantages as well as the advantages of your solution. If you try to disguise them it will give someone the opportunity to highlight them, giving the impression that either you are not being truthful or you have not considered the situation thoroughly. If your proposal involves major changes introduce them carefully, helping the people affected to accept and adjust to them.

Be prepared to listen to objections. Do not try to suppress objections. Give people the opportunity to explain their objections or you may create the impression you are trying to 'gloss over' flaws in your solution. You also deny yourself the opportunity to overcome the objections. Never argue with, or try to 'put down', someone who raises an objection. Your earlier analysis should have prepared you to overcome most objections.

Get them involved. It is still not too late to involve people to encourage their acceptance and commitment. For example, you could:

❑ Give them a role in the presentation, eg explaining how the solution affects their department.
❑ Give them a role in the implementation, either directly or in monitoring its effects.
❑ Allow them to contribute to your plan for implementation.

Demonstrate the importance of the problem. If you can show at the outset that the problem is important, either in its adverse effects or the benefits to be gained by its solution, people are likely to be more interested in hearing your ideas.

Appeal to their self-interest. Appealing to people's needs and desires is the best way to encourage them to listen and try to understand the implications of your proposals. Make a point of telling them at the beginning of the presentation how they will benefit. Express this again, in different ways, at any time you think you are losing their interest. Factors you can use include recognition, security, power, pride, self-respect and reward. A new management structure, for example, could be sold on its more equitable sharing of power, or greater efficiency leading to a reduced workload or larger bonuses.

Justify the resources you want to use. Solutions that tie up resources over long periods are often rejected on this criterion alone. Acceptance is more likely if your solution uses resources over a limited period or in short bursts. The greater the resources required the more carefully you need to explain the reasons for using them. Give as much proof as possible that your solution is cost-effective, eg hard facts about the return on investment.

Explain your solution effectively. The key to a successful presentation lies in the way you explain your solution. Make it easy to understand, show that it has been well thought out and that it is the best solution available under the circumstances.

Show enthusiasm for your solution. If you do not show enthusiasm for your solution neither will others. Enthusiasm can be infectious.

Be prepared to make concessions. One way of encouraging acceptance of a solution is to give way on certain points. This is particularly important where people expect negotiation or bargaining. Be prepared to vary your plan to accommodate individual needs that you had not considered. Prepare by identifying aspects of the solution that are not essential to achieving your objective. During negotiation you can 'trade' these for others which are essential.

Choose the right moment for your presentation. If you have a choice, make your presentation when your audience will be least distracted by other things (eg not just before lunch or at the end of the day) and when they will have time to consider your proposition fully before major interruptions (eg not just before a weekend or holiday).

The final step is to combine all this information into an effective presentation.

CREATING YOUR PRESENTATION

The way you present information is crucial to success. Aim to make your presentation clear, simple (as the subject allows) and to the point.

These guidelines will help ensure people understand you easily:

❏ Keep the presentation short and simple – don't confuse them with too much data or a very complex argument – but make sure that you cover all the important points.
❏ Avoid ambiguities.

❏ Prepare your presentation according to your audience's level of knowledge and understanding of the topics covered.
❏ Avoid any words or terms people may not understand, eg jargon and technical terms.

When the issues are complex concentrate on the key points. Leave the others for discussion later, if necessary, or for inclusion in an appendix to your report. State at the beginning of your presentation that this is what you intend to do. Most important of all, make your presentation a logical progression from the current circumstances, through obstacles and constraints, to the proposed actions and how they will achieve the objective. The following guidelines will help you use verbal and written presentations effectively.

Verbal presentations

The order in which you present your ideas is particularly important with verbal presentations. If you reveal your solution at the outset, for example, people may foresee disadvantages and raise objections before you have explained how you will handle the situation. This can lead to confusion and people may get the impression that your solution is impractical. First impressions are difficult to change. Following the steps below will help you structure your talk clearly, but you should still check regularly that everyone in the audience understands.

❏ State the overall objective in solving the problem.
❏ Describe the constraints on the situation.
❏ Briefly describe all the results that you felt were required and their relative importance.
❏ Briefly state all the options you considered without saying which you have chosen.
❏ Describe the criteria of evaluation you have used and their relative importance.

❏ State which option you have chosen, explaining why it is the best solution available, and the associated risks you have identified.
❏ Explain how the solution will be implemented.
❏ State how the results will be identified and measured.

This strategy uses the same methodical approach that you used in constructing the solution, making it easier to explain clearly and to deal with objections step-by-step.

Many people get anxious about making verbal presentations and this can be eased by thorough preparation and rehearsal. The following guidelines will help you create the right impression.

❏ Use unobtrusive keyword notes if you cannot remember all you want to say.
❏ Use visual aids if they help to get your ideas across more effectively.
❏ Speak confidently.
❏ Project your energy and enthusiasm through your voice (lively but not over-effusive), posture (upright but relaxed) and gestures (natural).
❏ Watch your audience for signs of how they are reacting to what you say (eg confused, impatient, inattentive) and respond accordingly.
❏ Answer questions carefully and succinctly (your preparation should have uncovered most of the likely questions).

Making verbal presentations is a skill that improves with practice. Rehearsal, preferably with an audience that can comment on your performance, will help you perfect a specific presentation.

Written presentations

Reports can vary from a single page outline to a large bound volume of 100 pages or more, but they should never contain unnecessary information. The features of a good report can be grouped under four headings.

1. *Contents*. A written report can be perused at will and digested at the reader's own pace, so there is a temptation not to worry about keeping the report short and simple. The easier you make it for people the more likely they are to read and accept your ideas. Interest will be sustained if you get to the point quickly.

2. *Structure*. This should help people understand your proposal. Follow the guidelines for verbal presentations above, presenting information step-by-step in a logical way. With complex issues only cover the main points in the body of the report and put supporting evidence and less significant information in appendices. If the body of the report is more than about 10 pages it's a good idea to give an abstract at the beginning covering the essential points, eg the problem, its effects and the recommended solution.

3. *Style*. The writing style should make the contents easy to read and understand. All the factors relating to jargon and so on mentioned above for verbal presentations also apply to reports. Sentences and paragraphs should be short and written in a conversational style unless the subject demands otherwise.

4. *Layout*. The layout of words on the page should give the appearance of being easy to follow and understand. Do not crowd pages, leave wide margins, give clear headings and emphasise important points.

Writing reports effectively is a skill that can be developed with practice. A good book on the subject will help you.

WHAT TO DO IF YOUR SOLUTION IS REJECTED

It is not uncommon for ideas to be rejected, particularly when they involve major change, are innovative or require extensive use of resources. If your idea is rejected you have a number of options:

❑   First, check that you presented your idea effectively. If not, it may be worth re-presenting it if you have the opportunity.

❑ Consider whether you can present the idea to someone else who can authorise its acceptance, or who could bring pressure to bear on the decision makers, eg those who will benefit most from your solution.

❑ Improve your solution to overcome the objections and then re-present it.

❑ Look for another solution, bearing in mind the reasons your first solution was rejected.

Trying to get your solution accepted can be frustrating and difficult. This is true especially where you are encroaching on other people's territory or where there is no existing yardstick to measure the likely outcome. If it is an idea you believe in, persevere. It often pays off.

IMPLEMENTING THE SOLUTION

Implementation is the culmination of your work in solving a problem and requires careful attention to detail. The three basic stages involved are planning and preparation, implementing and monitoring the action, and reviewing and analysing the success of the action.

PLANNING AND PREPARATION

Planning and preparation is the key to successful implementation. The more important the problem, or the more complex the actions required to solve it, the more thorough the planning and preparation required. The main tasks in planning and preparation are:

❏ Constructing a plan of action: the actions required, scheduling the actions, the resources required, measures to counter adverse consequences, management of the action, reviewing the plan.
❏ Arranging for resources to be made available at the appropriate time.
❏ Selecting, briefing and training those involved.

Constructing a plan of action

The plan of action describes what actions are required and how they will be implemented to ensure success. Unless the problem is simple or routine you need to construct a detailed plan. This involves systematically identifying and recording the elements described below.

The actions required

These must be identified fully and precisely otherwise the expected results will not be achieved. The outcome or effects of the actions must also be identified so that you will know when they have been completed successfully. Follow these steps to construct this part of the plan.

❏ State your overall objective.
❏ List the individual goals in the order in which they must be achieved to reach the objective.
❏ Identify what actions are required to achieve each goal, determine the sequence in which they need to be carried out, and record them alongside each goal.
❏ Define, in measurable terms, what a successful outcome will be for each action and add the details to the plan.

The sequence you choose for the various actions and goals is determined by a number of factors. Sometimes it is necessary to complete one action or set of actions before another can begin, eg laying a foundation before building a wall. Actions also have to run consecutively when they each use the same resource to its available capacity. On other occasions actions can run concurrently, eg when members of a team are each assigned a piece of equipment to test and evaluate.

With all but the very simplest plans it is wise to use a diagram to represent the sequence of actions and how they contribute to the overall objective. This helps to show how the actions interact and to reveal areas of possible conflict. Actions should be fitted together as closely as possible, to prevent wastage of resources, while allowing some margin for overrun. To do this you need to prepare a time schedule for the actions.

Scheduling the actions

To create a time schedule first you identify the time required to complete each action. By representing this information on a diagram you can see clearly at what stage, relative to the start time, each action will commence and finish, and determine the total time required to achieve the objective. Simple plans can be represented by a chart that uses bars to show the sequence and duration of the actions, as shown in Figure 10.1.

More complex plans require a more flexible structure, like chain diagrams (see page 54) or flowcharts. Diagrams help you arrange the actions in a way that makes the best use of time and other resources. For example, if two actions each require two days' use of an excavator that can be hired only on a weekly basis, ideally these actions should be scheduled for the same week. When completed, the diagram also shows which actions are most crucial to complete on time (eg draining a flooded site before the excavators move in), and how a delay or time-saving in completing one action will affect all the others (eg bad

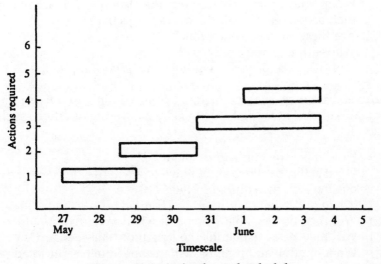

Figure 10.1 *A simple work schedule*

weather may delay the commencement of one action and have a knock-on effect).

In drawing up a schedule it is important not to be over-optimistic in the time you allow for each action. Additional time is required to accommodate delays and unforeseen obstacles, particularly with actions that must be completed on time or are susceptible to delays. Methods for identifying potential delays are described later (page 124).

The resources required

Resources to complete each action have to be defined precisely along a number of parameters, including the type, amount and time they are required. Each resource is considered individually.

Time is easily overlooked but it can be a key resource in some situations, eg completing the installation of new manufacturing plant before the end of the annual 'shutdown' period. It can be defined by answering this type of question:

❑ What time is available before the deadline for achieving each action, each goal, the overall objective?
❑ Are these timings compatible?
❑ Whose time is required?
❑ Will this time be spent within normal working hours?

Human resources may be required from within and outside the organisation. These can be defined by answering questions such as:

❑ How many people will be required?
❑ What skills, qualities and knowledge will they need to carry out the actions required of them?
❑ When and where will they be required?
❑ Will they be available when and where required?
❑ Will they be available for the length of time required?
❑ What briefing and training will they need to be able to carry out their tasks effectively?

Financial resources can be defined through questions such as:

❑ How much money will be needed?
❑ In what form, eg cash, cheque, foreign currency?
❑ How will it be acquired, eg loan, grant, endowment?
❑ What will be the source, eg profits, merchant bank, share-holders, local or central government?
❑ How will it be used and is this compatible with the source, eg if it is a development grant does the plan use it appropriately?
❑ When and where will it be required?
❑ Will it be available when and where required?
❑ Does it need to be repaid and when?
❑ Will it be recouped, how and when, eg through increased profits?
❑ Will there be additional cost in using this money, eg interest or handling charges?
❑ Have the costs of all other resources been included?

Materials may fall into a number of categories including consumables, raw materials and equipment (for temporary or permanent use). The following questions help define material requirements:

❑ What type of materials will be required?
❑ If capital equipment is required, how will it be financed, eg lease, loan?
❑ What are the specifications of the materials required, eg quality, size?
❑ What wastage is likely to occur?
❑ In what quantities are they required?
❑ When and where will they be required?
❑ Will they be available when and where required?
❑ Will transport be required?
❑ What handling (human and mechanical) will be required?
❑ Will storage space be required, where, how much, for how long and will it be available?

Storage requirements can be defined by asking questions such as:

❏ How much space will be required?
❏ Where will the space be required?
❏ Does it have to be of a particular type (eg covered, with amenities) or particular dimensions?
❏ When will the space be required and for how long?

Information may form a part of the human resource (eg expert advice or skills) but it can also be a resource in its own right (eg renting a mailing list for a direct mail campaign). The following type of questions help define information requirements:

❏ What specific information will be required?
❏ Is this information available from within the organisation or does it have to be bought-in?
❏ Where specifically is it available?
❏ When and where will it be required?
❏ Will it be available when and where required?
❏ How long will it be required?

When you are calculating the resources required to implement a solution it is vital not to under-estimate. A shortage could disrupt implementation completely and possibly incur heavy penalties, eg having to pay a consultant for doing nothing while she's waiting for the installation of a piece of equipment. Sometimes you have to adapt your plan of action to suit the availability of resources.

Once you have made a complete list of the resource requirements, draw up a schedule of resources showing how and when they will be requested, from whom, when and where they are to be delivered or made available and, where relevant, for how long they will be required. It is important to allow sufficient time between ordering and the required delivery date to ensure that any delay will not disrupt your time schedule.

Measures to counter adverse consequences

You have considered the areas of risk and possible side-effects when constructing and evaluating your solution. You have adapted it to try to minimise the adverse consequences. Now you need to identify everything that could go wrong during implementation, and devise countermeasures. This includes even minor problems, eg a temporary power cut, which prevents the use of equipment.

The steps involved are similar to those used to evaluate and minimise the risks associated with the solution, only more detailed. There are certain features of a plan of action which make it more susceptible to something going wrong. To identify these and make provision to deal with them, examine your plan step-by-step:

EXERCISE

Identify everything that could go wrong. Are there areas where, for example:

- ☐ Timing is crucial, eg with delays, could a deadline be missed?
- ☐ A slippage in timing could bring subsequent actions into conflict, eg so that they simultaneously require the same resource?
- ☐ Two or more activities coincide, eg will they interfere with each other?
- ☐ There is no way of predicting what may happen, eg because of lack of knowledge or experience?
- ☐ There is heavy reliance on facilities or equipment, eg could they fail?
- ☐ There is heavy reliance on the cooperation and efforts of people, eg will they perform as required?
- ☐ All available resources in a particular category are being used, eg could an unexpected event require their more urgent use elsewhere?

❑ External factors could affect the actions required (eg withdrawal of labour in a national dispute) or the effectiveness of the results (eg a change in market needs)?

Analyse and evaluate the consequences:

❑ What are the effects if this happens?
❑ How serious are they?
❑ What is their relative seriousness?
❑ What is the probability of them happening (low, medium or high)?

Define how you could recognise trouble as early as possible, eg through the detection of unexpected variance in predicted events.

Devise countermeasures where possible to either prevent the cause or minimise its effects.

Incorporate the method of recognition and the appropriate counter-measure into your plan.

Adverse consequences with the combined highest probability and greatest seriousness should be tackled first. Every effort must be made to include provisions in the plan to counter them effectively. Even if time is short and requires extensive work, you can only afford to omit minor adverse consequences with a low probability. Problems may not arise during implementation but if they do you need a plan of appropriate countermeasures or you risk jeopardising the rest of the plan.

Management of the action

Unless the solution is very simple or routine you must specify how the implementation will be monitored and controlled. Human resources must be appropriately led and managed, their progress measured at specific intervals and appropriate action taken to correct any variation from the plan. The following steps help specify how to manage the implementation

EXERCISE

Identify actions which require on-the-job supervision and monitoring, eg where individuals have little experience of the actions required of them or the outcome is highly variable.

Identify the stages at which progress should be measured, eg upon completion of individual goals or major activities, at critical phases.

Specify exactly what results are expected to have been achieved at these stages.

Specify how and by whom the actual results will be measured.

Ensure that appropriate measures to correct any variance between the expected and the actual results are specified in the plan.

The stages you identify for measuring progress are, in effect, deadlines for achieving specific results. These must be stated as a specific time or date in the overall time schedule. Unspecific or woolly deadlines make implementation difficult to manage and can lead to disaster. The frequency of measuring progress is dependent upon a number of factors:

❑ What is practical, eg economical and not interfering significantly with progress.
❑ The rate at which the situation is likely to change, eg major building works compared with delicate negotiations over a couple of days.
❑ The seriousness of potential variation from the plan, eg points at which unnoticed mistakes in the construction of a distillation plant could make its operation dangerous.

Provision should also be made to monitor the solution once it has been implemented, so that any unforeseen adverse consequences arising in the longer term can be detected. For example, has a change in the system created a bottleneck in processing work, or resulted in undue pressure on one individual or department?

Reviewing the plan

Finally, you need to check the plan to ensure:

❑ The actions listed will achieve the various goals and the overall objective.
❑ Your time schedule is workable and can accommodate unexpected delays.
❑ Your estimation of resources is accurate.
❑ The plan for managing the action will help keep it on course.

Drawing up a plan of action is the most crucial stage in ensuring efficient implementation. It must be accurate and thorough. This plan provides a blueprint for the remaining stages of implementation.

Arranging resources

When you were planning resources you will have identified what resources are required and in what amounts. You should also have drawn up a schedule showing how and when they would be requested, from whom, when and where they were to be delivered and, if appropriate, for how long they would be required. Lead times for supply will also have been identified. This information can be translated easily into a plan of the resource 'suppliers', the time when resources will need to be ordered or requested, in what amounts, and so on.

Selecting, briefing and training those involved

Your plan of action provides most of the information you require at this stage. What you do is similar to delegating a task to someone. There are two or three steps: selecting people, briefing them and, if necessary, providing training.

1. *Selection.* You need people with the skills, qualities and knowledge necessary to carry out the various tasks. First you identify the ideal attributes for carrying out these tasks effectively, both in what is required and in what should be avoided.

Then you can construct profiles of the ideal candidate for each group of tasks. Selection consists of finding the best match to this ideal among the people available. Frequently there will be at least some aspects of your plan for which the people readily available are not ideally suited. If the discrepancy is large it may be necessary to hire people with the appropriate attributes. At other times the shortfall can be overcome by careful briefing or specific training.

Once you have selected people, you need a plan of what each person has to do, the results they will be expected to achieve and what responsibilities they have for achieving these results. You will use this to brief them and may also prepare notes for them to use.

2. *Briefing*. This is often the final step before a plan is implemented. People need to know and understand what they have to do. As in any other type of communication it must be planned and executed carefully. The following steps can help.

❑ Give individuals reasonable advance warning of what will be required of them.

❑ Prepare your briefing carefully so that it is clear, comprehensive and can be understood easily by everyone involved (the guidelines on presentations, page 114, will help you).

❑ After the briefing, check that everyone has understood what they are required to do by asking them to explain your instructions in their own words.

Your instructions should state clearly the responsibilities of each individual and the scope of their authority in carrying out their tasks. It is important to give a level of authority that allows people to use their initiative. If they foresee a problem arising, for example, they may need some freedom to act immediately.

The way you communicate your message is very important. Some people may have a different view of the situation and different attitudes to your own, particularly if they have not been involved in finding and evaluating solutions. The guide-lines in Chapter 9 will help encourage their cooperation and commitment.

3. *Training*. If people with the appropriate skills are not readily available you need to compare the advantages and disadvantages of training them versus hiring other people. For example, training could provide individuals with skills that are of value in other aspects of their work. On the other hand, hiring a consultant may create a valuable business contact.

Once people have been briefed on what they have to do the plan of action can be implemented.

IMPLEMENTING AND MONITORING THE ACTION

Once action has been initiated it has to be supervised and monitored. If there is variation from the plan it may be necessary to take corrective action immediately.

Supervising the action ensures that individuals carry out their tasks efficiently according to the plan.

Monitoring progress helps to identify whether or not the results being achieved are meeting the planned requirements, and if not why not. A decision can then be made on the action required to put the plan back on course. Reviewing the overall achievement once the plan has progressed significantly will indicate how well it is achieving the objective. If there are major discrepancies it suggests that the plan is inadequate and needs to be revised.

Taking corrective action may involve implementing the appropriate countermeasure laid down in the plan, or taking unplanned action to counter unforeseen problems. If time has been lost in completing one activity, for example, other activities may have to be completed more quickly than planned to meet a deadline. Minor problems that are unlikely to recur may not require any action. Major faults in the plan may make it necessary to abandon implementation if no appropriate corrective action is possible.

These three processes must be maintained until the plan is completed.

REVIEWING AND ANALYSING THE OUTCOME

When the plan has been completed and the solution implemented it is important to measure and analyse its success. This tells you how effective the solution has been and how useful it will be in solving similar problems in the future. There are three stages involved.

1. *Measuring success.* Right at the beginning of solving the problem you identified the objective you wanted to achieve and stated it in measurable terms. Now you need to compare the results achieved with those you set out to achieve. Sometimes it is necessary to measure the results regularly over a period of time to see if the initial results are being maintained, eg when the novelty of a new system has worn off you need to know if people are still using it efficiently. Changes in the effectiveness of the solution also can occur with changes in the objective, eg in a fast moving market a 'new' product does not remain new for long.

2. *Analysing discrepancies.* If the outcome falls short of, or exceeds, the predicted results you need to know why. You might want to take further action to overcome a shortfall in results. If your expectations have been exceeded and you identify the reason perhaps you can use this to improve results even further. Identifying the cause of discrepancies can also give you an idea of your strengths and weaknesses in problem solving.

3. *Taking further action.* This may be required for a number of reasons. Initial results could be inadequate; maybe results can't be maintained without intervention; perhaps the goal posts have moved and results do not meet the new targets. To decide what further action is required you need to define new objectives and

any associated obstacles – a new problem for you to solve and the process has come full circle.

Implementation makes your problem solving efforts tangible. If you get the results you wanted you can congratulate yourself on a job well done (although there is always room for improvement). If your solution is not quite as successful as you had hoped it's an ideal opportunity to become a better problem solver by finding out why.

11

YOUR PROBLEM-SOLVING
CHECKLIST

This chapter provides a quick reference summary. Solving problems effectively involves a number of processes using a variety of mental skills. The experienced problem solver knows instinctively what steps to follow, what skills to apply at each stage and what techniques are available to help. This comes with practice. The following summary will help you become familiar with the different stages of problem solving and when and how to apply particular skills and techniques.

HINDRANCES TO PROBLEM SOLVING

There are wide-ranging factors that can hinder your problem solving. To avoid their effects you need to:

❑ Be aware constantly of the factors that are likely to affect you.
❑ Learn the techniques available to overcome or avoid their effects and apply them when necessary.

INVOLVING OTHERS IN SOLVING THE PROBLEM

Some problems are solved more effectively in a group.

The more times you answer 'yes' to the following questions the more appropriate it is to tackle the problem as a group:

❏ Can the problem be defined in many different ways?
❏ Is information from many different sources required?
❏ Is it a very specialised problem?
❏ Does the problem have implications for many people?
❏ Are there likely to be many possible solutions?
❏ Is it a complex problem with many different aspects?
❏ Will a solution need to be agreed by others?

The deciding question will always be: 'Are suitable and relevant people available to work together in solving this problem?' There are a number of techniques designed specifically for solving problems as a group. Even if you do not have access to these they can teach you a lot about working with others on a problem.

RECOGNISING AND DEFINING A PROBLEM

This is a key stage. To recognise problems effectively you need to:

❏ Be aware of the areas in which problems may arise.
❏ Establish specific methods of detection:
  – monitor performance against agreed standards;
  – observe people to detect any behaviour reflecting an underlying problem;
  – listen to people so that you are aware of their concerns;
  – regularly review and compare current and past performance and behaviour to detect gradual deterioration.

To define problems effectively you need to distinguish between maintenance and achievement problems and analyse them differently.

Maintenance problems

❑ Identify and record all aspects of the deviation from the norm (the Kepner-Tregoe approach is a good method).
❑ Analyse the information to identify possible causes.
❑ Test each possible cause against the known facts to identify the actual cause.
❑ Define in a similar way to achievement problems.

Achievement problems

❑ Identify all the objectives you may want to achieve, eg in terms of 'How to ...?'
❑ Select the 'How to ...?' statements that most accurately represent your problem.
❑ For each one, list the characteristics of the current and desired situations.
❑ Add details of any obstacles that may prevent you achieving the desired situation.
❑ Add details of the needs of other people who are affected.

DECIDING IF AND WHEN TO ACT

Not all problems are important enough to merit the resources required to solve them. Even when they do, it is sometimes better to wait rather than to act immediately. Answering the following questions will tell you if the problem requires action and whether it would be best to act now or wait.

❑ Will the problem solve itself?
❑ Are the effects significant enough to merit the resources that may be required to solve the problem?

❏ Is the problem diminishing? (*wait*)
❏ Are the obstacles diminishing? (*wait*)
❏ Will the cause subside? (*wait*)
❏ Is the problem having serious effects? (*act*)
❏ Is the problem growing? (*act*)
❏ Are the obstacles growing? (*act*)
❏ Is there an imminent deadline? (*act*)

FINDING POSSIBLE SOLUTIONS

Achievement problems usually have many possible solutions while maintenance problems have one or a limited number of solutions. The cause of a maintenance problem might be identified when defining the problem, or it may require further research and the testing of hypotheses about the cause. To find possible solutions follow these stages:

1. *Identify the relevant information*, initially based on your problem definition:

❏ What information is needed?
❏ Why is it needed?
❏ Where can it be obtained?
❏ How reliable will it be?
❏ How can it be obtained?

2. *Gather and record the information*. This should be a systematic process and remember to check the accuracy of information.

3. *Represent the information* in a model of the problem. This gives it structure and helps in your search for solutions. At this stage it may be necessary to look for other possible causes of maintenance problems.

4. *Define criteria of effectiveness*. This gives direction to your search for solutions. List the characteristics of an 'ideal' solution:

❑ What benefits are you seeking?
❑ What obstacles or causes have to be dealt with?
❑ What are the constraints on the situation?
❑ What will be acceptable to those involved or affected?
❑ What level of risk is acceptable?

Some of these questions can be answered fully only after you have found possible solutions.

5. *Construct courses of action* to solve the problem. This involves finding ways of achieving the criteria of effectiveness you have defined. The possible solutions are modified and refined to take account of factors that could influence their effectiveness. Identify these by asking questions such as:

❑ What could go wrong?
❑ Are there factors over which you have no control?
❑ Could the objectives change?
❑ Could the obstacles become more intractable?
❑ Could new obstacles arise?
❑ Could this solution create an opportunity that can be exploited at the same time?

EVALUATING SOLUTIONS

Deciding which of the possible solutions will be most effective is a systematic process that can be divided into stages:

1. *Involve others*:

❑ When you have a formal obligation to consult them.
❑ When you require additional information to help in the evaluation.
❑ When you require their expert skills.
❑ When you need their commitment.

2. *Define the 'ideal' solution*:

❏ Results required:
   – benefits in terms of the objective;
   – dealing effectively with obstacles or causes;
   – acceptance of the solution by other people.
❏ Constraints:
   – limits of resources
   – minimum results acceptable;
   – maximum disadvantages that can be tolerated.

The results required are given numerical values according to their relative importance. Where the outcome is uncertain you need to calculate probabilities.

3. *Eliminate unviable solutions*, ie those not meeting the constraints.

4. *Evaluate the remaining solutions*, ie estimate how well each one fits the ideal solution. The ideal fit on each dimension of the results required is given an arbitrary value. Disadvantages are given a negative value. Each solution is evaluated by multiplying its relative fit by the relative value of each result. The best solution is the one with the highest aggregate score.

5. *Assess the risks* associated with this solution:

❏ Is the information used in the construction and evaluation of the solution accurate?
❏ If not, could this put the success of the solution in jeopardy and how?
❏ What could happen if the implementation does not go as planned?
❏ What are the chances of these things happening?
❏ What would be the effects?
❏ How severe would they be?

If the risks are unacceptable and cannot be reduced by adapting the solution it must be rejected and the next highest scoring solution assessed. Continue this process until you find a solution involving acceptable risk.

6. *Take action*. Finally, take the decision to implement the solution. The problem will remain unsolved unless you commit to taking action.

GETTING A SOLUTION ACCEPTED

To encourage people to accept your solution, and to gain their commitment to its successful implementation, first you need to draw up a plan for implementing the solution (see the next section) and then:

1. *Identify areas of possible opposition*. Consider:

❏ How the solution could adversely affect the people involved.
❏ What they expect or need from the solution and what it will give them.
❏ Their feelings about the nature of the problem and your solution.
❏ Their relationship with, and perception of, you.
❏ What the solution requires of them.

2. *Prepare a presentation* which optimises the chances of your solution being accepted and supported:

❏ Incorporate measures to counter opposition.
❏ Get people involved and interested.
❏ Appeal to their self-interest.
❏ Justify your proposed use of resources.
❏ Explain your solution effectively.
❏ Be prepared to make concessions.

3. *Deliver your presentation effectively* (whether written or spoken):

❑ Choose the right moment.
❑ Make it clear and easy to understand.
❑ Show enthusiasm for the solution.

Persevere until you succeed, either by improving your presentation or your solution, presenting it to someone else, or by looking for a different solution.

IMPLEMENTING THE SOLUTION

To ensure that your solution is implemented successfully, and achieves the results you expect, follow these steps:

1. *Plan and prepare* to implement the solution:

❑ Draw up a plan of action;
  – the actions required;
  – a schedule of actions;
  – the resources required (what, how much and when);
  – measures to counter adverse consequences;
  – management of the action.
❑ Review the plan to ensure that it is adequate and accurate.
❑ Arrange for resources to be made available at the appropriate time.
❑ Select, brief and train those involved to ensure they have the appropriate information, skills and qualities required to implement the action successfully.

2. *Implement* action **and monitor** the situation:

❑ Supervise the action.
❑ Monitor its implementation and effects.
❑ Keep it on track by countering unexpected delays, faults and obstacles.

3. *Review and analyse* the success of the action:

❑ Compare the outcome of the action with the expected results.

❑ Identify any discrepancies (positive or negative) and analyse them to identify the causes.

❑ Take further action if necessary, eg to correct a shortfall or to maintain current results.

You can learn a lot about problem solving from books but practice is the best way to develop your skills. This book should have given you a wider perspective on 'problems'; they are not limited to the major crises that we commonly imagine. Any challenging situation can be turned into a problem-solving opportunity. When you approach everyday situations in this way you will find the most rewarding aspect of becoming a better problem solver is feeling more in control; more effective in turning day-to-day events to your advantage. Good problem solvers seem to have a knack of getting what they want.

FURTHER READING

Adams, James L (1979) *Conceptual Blockbusting*, WW Norton, New York.

Bird, Malcolm (1993) *Problem Solving Techniques That Really Work*, Piatkus Books, London.

Buzan, Tony with Buzan, Barry (1993) *The Mind Map Book*, BBC Publications, London.

Chang, Richard Y and Kelly, P Keith (1995) *Step-by-step Problem-Solving: Ensure Problems Get (and Stay) Solved*, Kogan Page, London.

Cox, Geof (1995) *Practical Guide to Solving Business Problems*, Pitman/The Institute of Management, London.

Delaney, William A (1984) *Tricks of the Manager's Trade*, AMA-COM, New York.

Goman, Carol Kinsey (1989) *Creative Thinking in Business*, Kogan Page, London.

Koberg, Don and Bagnall, Jim (1974) *The Universal Traveler*, William Kaufmann, Los Altos, California.

Koestler, Arthur (1989) *The Act of Creation*. Penguin, Harmondsworth.

McKim, Robert H (1980) *Experiences in Visual Thinking*, Brooks-Cole, Monterey, California.

Pokras, Sandy (1990) *Systematic Problem Solving and Decision Making*, Kogan Page, London.

Robson, Mike (1993) *Problem Solving in Groups*. Gower, Aldershot.

Sowrey, Trevor (1988) *The Generation of Ideas for New Products*, Kogan Page, London.

Weiss, Donald H (1988) *Creative Problem Solving*, AMACOM, New York.

Weiss, W H (1986) *The Supervisor's Problem Solver*, AMACOM, New York.

Wilson, Graham (1993) *Problem Solving and Decision Making*, Kogan Page in association with The Association for Management Education and Development, London.

INDEX